COUNTERCULTURAL WORSHIP

Smyth & Helwys Publishing, Inc.
6316 Peake Road
Macon, Georgia 31210-3960
1-800-747-3016
©2016 by Mark G. McKim
All rights reserved.

Library of Congress Cataloging-in-Publication Data

Names: McKim, Mark G., 1961- author.
Title: Countercultural worship : a plea to evangelicals in a secular age /
by Mark G. McKim.
Description: Macon, GA : Smyth & Helwys Publishing, 2016.
Identifiers: LCCN 2016008799 | ISBN 9781573128735 (pbk. : alk. paper)
Subjects: LCSH: Public worship. | Secularism. | Evangelicalism.
Classification: LCC BV15 .M375 2016 | DDC 264--dc23
LC record available at https://lccn.loc.gov/2016008799

Unless otherwise noted the Scripture quotations contained herein are from the New Revised Standard Version Bible.

Disclaimer of Liability: With respect to statements of opinion or fact available in this work of nonfiction, Smyth & Helwys Publishing Inc. nor any of its employees, makes any warranty, express or implied, or assumes any legal liability or responsibility for the accuracy or completeness of any information disclosed, or represents that its use would not infringe privately-owned rights.

COUNTERCULTURAL WORSHIP

A PLEA TO EVANGELICALS IN A SECULAR AGE

Mark G. McKim

Also by Mark McKim

Emil Brunner: A Bibliography

*Christian Theology for a Secular Society:
Singing the Lord's Song in a Strange Land*

For Mom,
who first taught me about and modeled
God's self-sacrificing love.
Your encouragement and support have never failed.

Acknowledgments

I express my deep gratitude to the following:

The congregation of First Baptist Church, Regina, Saskatchewan, Canada, for their support of the academic side of my life, their understanding that the life of the mind can be offered as service to God, and especially their granting me a semester of sabbatical leave in 2010 during which much of the initial research for this book was undertaken;

The Fellows of Regent's Park College, University of Oxford, for electing me as a Visiting Fellow of the Senior Common Room during my sabbatical;

Ms. Shuana Niessen, Managing Editor, Faculty of Education, University of Regina, and Dr. Esther Weins, former professor of English at the Canadian Bible College, Regina, Saskatchewan, for their careful proofreading and helpful comments on content.

Contents

Preface: Warning to the Reader ... ix

Chapter 1: What Is Worship? ... 1

Chapter 2: What Is Secularization and How Has Evangelical Worship Been Secularized? ... 31

Chapter 3: Principles for an Evangelical Theology of Worship ... 55

Chapter 4: What an Evangelical Common Worship Service Looks Like ... 83

Chapter 5: Music and Common Worship ... 127

Chapter 6: Resources for Common Worship that Is Not Secularized ... 139

Preface:
Warning to the Reader

You may have heard the Latin phrase *Caveat Emptor*, "Let the buyer beware." I begin with another Latin phrase: *Caveat Lector*, "Let the reader beware." Those beginning this book are forewarned that it may puzzle, disturb, and even anger some readers.

For some it will be puzzling because they have never reflected, been taught how to reflect, or even been invited to reflect on what happens when they join with other Christians for worship. For the first time, they may find themselves questioning long-established and familiar practices. Such questioning can be troubling. But I urge you not to be afraid to ask questions or to be puzzled. Being puzzled and asking questions are often good things for a follower of Jesus Christ. Remember that the disciples were often puzzled and frequently asked Jesus for explanations. And just as they did then, honest, seeking questions today often lead to a better understanding of Scripture and a more thoughtful, deeper, mature following of Christ.

I am most concerned about those who may find themselves feeling angry when they read this book. It is rarely easy to hear familiar practices and routines being criticized or questioned. That is particularly so for matters of faith because there is so much at stake. And it is precisely because I believe there is so much at stake that I have written this book—as an evangelical, for evangelicals.

The word *evangelical* has been misused, misunderstood, and misappropriated so often in recent decades that it needs some explanation. "Evangelical" has been linked with or attached to everything from a particular American political party, capitalism, and anti-gun control lobbyists to unquestioning political, economic, and military support for the nation of Israel. "Evangelical" has been used in the popular media to describe Qu'ran-burning preachers and a wide variety of conspiracy theorists. Churches describe themselves as "evangelical" because every worship service ends with an "altar call," even though they may be almost completely disconnected from their culture and neighbours. None of this would have made much sense to those Protestant Christians who were first called evangelicals in early eighteenth- to mid-nineteenth-century England, women and men such as Anthony Ashley-Cooper (Earl of Shaftesbury), John Howard, Hannah More, John Newton, Selina Hastings (Countess of Huntingdon), John and Charles Wesley, George Whitefield, and William Wilberforce. *Historic* evangelicalism, as it originated in this period, was distinguished by several features, including

- a high view of the authority of Scripture as being the final authority in matters of faith and practice, and the guide for living daily life;
- a consequent heavy stress on the importance of expository and doctrinal preaching;
- a life formed to being like Jesus, attuned to God's will, usually through the employment of such disciplines including but not limited to the private study of Scripture and prayer;
- emphasis on the need for personal repentance and acceptance of Jesus as Lord;
- emphasis on evangelism, witness, and foreign missions, matched by
- work toward Social Reform (Howard advocated for prison reform; More was a pioneer in education for children; Lord Shaftesbury led the campaign for improvement in working conditions for factory workers, banning boys of less than ten and women and girls from mines, and for improvement of the condition of mental patients; Newton and Wilberforce were major figures in the campaign against slavery);
- serious engagement with—which often meant deeply challenging—the culture and mores of eighteenth- and nineteenth-century British society;
- an approach to both corporate and private worship that was God centred (theocentric), Christ centred (christocentric), and Scripture centred (bibliocentric).

Let it be clear that I happily and wholeheartedly agree with these emphases. I identify myself as a *historic* evangelical. I was raised in the evangelical tradition, but I also consciously choose to identify with that tradition.

This book reflects a lover's quarrel with one particular aspect of evangelicalism—corporate worship—and a plea to my fellow evangelicals that we "do" worship much better than is often the case. I am convinced that what happens in many evangelical churches on Sunday morning has become deeply secularized. The focus has shifted, often unwittingly, from

God, whom we know best in Jesus Christ, to ourselves: our needs, our desires, our preferences. While God may often enough be mentioned, in reality God is not the centre of attention. That this is happening in the midst of an increasingly secular Western society where God is also marginalized—both in the public square and the day-to-day lives of most citizens—is deeply troubling. The kind of worship that happens week in and week out often represents our being shaped and moulded by our culture rather than our being the deeply counter-cultural vanguard of the kingdom of God. We are in danger of becoming chaplains to the culture, a vaguely "religious" reflection of the values and beliefs of our society.

Something must be done. This book represents a small contribution to the ongoing and, thankfully, increasingly widespread conversation among evangelical Christians toward that end.

Caveat Lector—Let the reader beware.

Dr. Mark G. McKim

Chapter 1

What Is Worship?

Worship. It is a word used often among evangelical Christians, but, much like the word "evangelical," worship has become a slippery word indeed—incredibly hard to define or hold on to. Like many such "church words," it is often simply assumed that everyone agrees and understands what the word "worship" means. In fact, not everyone agrees or even understands. It is commonplace, for instance, to be told that "worship begins in the sanctuary at 11:00 a.m. and ends at about noon." By itself, this suggests that worship is something that is confined to a particular place for a specific hour or two on Sunday morning and has nothing to do with the rest of the week. In some churches on Sunday morning, the first twenty or thirty minutes of singing choruses—usually while standing—is called worship. This of course prompts the question of what is going on for the remainder of the time the congregation spends together. The same word—*worship*—is used to refer both to a gathering of Christians around a bonfire at a church camp, consisting entirely of singing gospel hymns, and to morning prayer according to the Anglican Book of Common Prayer.

Much like the word "evangelical," the word "worship" gets applied loosely and imprecisely to so many different things that it can signify almost anything and everything, which results in its meaning nothing in particular.

The most important step in trying to think clearly, deeply, and carefully about anything is to know precisely *what* one is thinking about. In other words, we need to define our terms so that we understand what the words we are using actually mean. Words—and what they mean—are important, critical in fact. That should not come as a surprise to those who confess Jesus Christ as Lord. He was called *the* Word, and what *he* meant and means was and remains of critical importance.

The Meaning of the Word "Worship"

In the Bible, a variety of different words and phrases is used to denote worship. These include terms that come into English as "adoration," "to serve," "to prostrate oneself," and "to seek the face of God." Together, the biblical words and phrases, set in context, communicate an attitude of service, submission, reverential respect, and both recognition and acceptance of God's sovereignty or lordship. The various terms are used sometimes to refer to a reverent, pious approach taken in all of life and sometimes, more specifically, to corporate worship, particularly in settings like the temple in Jerusalem.

Our English word "worship" derives from both Anglian and Saxon and means "the condition of being worthy." To worship means to acknowledge the worth or value of something or someone. Specifically, Christian worship means the acknowledgment and acceptance of the supreme worth of the God whom we have come to know best in Jesus Christ, submission to and reverential respect for this God, and, most important, acceptance of Christ's lordship demonstrated in obedience to him.

Four Circles of Worship

Using this understanding, the biblical witness can be understood as communicating four concentric circles of Christian worship. Each circle is larger than and encompasses the one before it. In practice, there is a good deal of overlap of the circles, as they merge one into another. But they are distinguishable one from the other, at least for purposes of discussion.

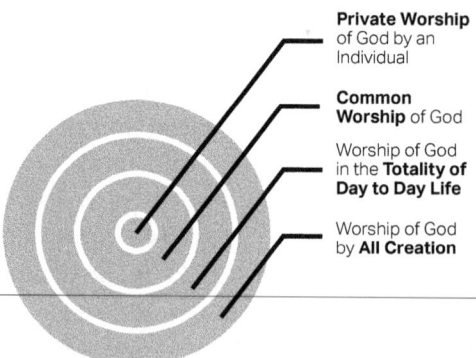

The largest, outer, circle depicts the worship of God by all creation, which includes everything outside of God who is, of course, uncreated—the universe and whatever may exist beyond it. Again and again the images we are given in the Bible look forward to a day when *all* creation will worship God. Isaiah pictures a day when God makes for all people a banquet, a day when the people will rejoice in God's provision, acknowledging that God has fulfilled his ancient promises:

> On this mountain the LORD of hosts
> > will make for all peoples
> a feast of rich food, a feast of
> > well aged wines . . . .
> It will be said on that day,
> > Lo, this is our God; we have
> > Waited for him, so that he
> > Might save us.
> This is the LORD for whom we have waited;
> > Let us be glad and rejoice in his
> > Salvation. (Isa 25:6, 9)

Isaiah also records God's promise, quoted centuries later by Paul in his letter to the Romans:

> By myself I have sworn,
> > From my mouth has gone forth in righteousness
> > a word that shall not return:
> "To me every knee shall bow,
> > every tongue shall swear." (Isa 45:23)

Paul writes to the Philippians,

> at the name of Jesus every knee [will] bend,
> > in heaven and on earth and under the earth,
> and every tongue [will] confess
> > that Jesus is Lord,
> > to the glory of God the Father. (Phil 2:10-11)

John, in his revelation at Patmos, recorded a vision in which *every* creature sings the praise of God the Father and his Son, Jesus:

> Then I heard every creature in heaven and on earth and under the earth
> and in the sea, and that is in them, singing,
> > "To the one seated on the throne
> > > and to the Lamb
> > be blessing and honor and glory
> > > and might
> > forever and ever! "(Rev 5:13)

All of these are pictures of the great cosmic hymn of worship, the true "music of the spheres." The biblical witness is that *only* when creatures find their place in this never-ending, all-consuming worship do they find fulfillment and joy. *Only* when the God whom we know best in Jesus is Lord of *all* of life and worshipped as such is any creature whole and fulfilled. "Life," as C. F. D. Moule wrote, "has no other purpose than to be rendered up to God in adoration and gratitude."[1] Moreover, "Ultimately, life has no meaning at all unless it is all for God and unless its whole aim is worship."[2] This is why pictures we are given in Scripture of the Kingdom, God's rule and will realized, are those of ongoing, never-ending, eternal worship. It is why Paul opens his letter to the Ephesians by observing that those who are redeemed ". . . live for the praise of his [God's] glory" (Eph 1:12). The whole purpose and meaning of creation is to worship God. Humans, and all the rest of creation, were created for worship, and without it we are incomplete and lack purpose and meaning. Indeed, "worship is the highest and most fulfilling act of which a human being is capable; it is that experience in which we in fact become most truly human . . . ."[3] There is, as Christopher Ellis puts it, "no higher calling than . . . to worship God . . . . [Worship] should be the summit of our human experience."[4]

All the other circles of worship are intended to join us to this largest circle of worship, so that our hearts, minds, bodies, and souls are fully engaged with the worship of God. *All* the other circles of worship may be thought of as practicing for that moment when we will join the largest circle of worship perfectly and eternally.

The second largest of the four circles represents the totality of day-to-day ordinary human life. In this "big picture" sense, *all* of life is to be worship. To accept the lordship of Christ means that *every* part of life is to be subject to his rule, *every* aspect of life is to reflect the acknowledgment and acceptance of the supreme worth of the God whom we have come to know best in Jesus Christ, *every* moment of life is be submitted to him with reverential respect. "Worship" as David Peterson writes, "is a comprehensive category describing the Christian's total existence."[5] In this, the second biggest circle of worship, life is a preparation, a rehearsal, for what humans were designed for and which the redeemed will spend eternity engaged in: worship. "Worship is a total-life orientation . . . ."[6] Very often among evangelicals, salvation is seen as the heart of what Christianity is about. This is an inaccurate, attenuated understanding of Scripture. Christianity is about seeing the Kingdom, God's will or rule realized, and when that Kingdom comes in full and all is set to rights, the centre of all things will once again be the worship of God. Then and only then when "the aim and purpose of human beings . . . to recognize and celebrate their creaturehood by recognizing that only God is God and they are not . . . [will] creation [be] finally in order . . . ."[7] Ben Witherington III expresses this well when he writes, "worship is the ultimate aim and goal of salvation. Salvation is but a means to an end, not an end in itself."[8] Salvation leads to the ultimate goal, which is worship. As Witherington puts it, "[Worship] completes the intended life cycle of all creatures great and small. The chief end of humankind and human history is *not* the salvation of all persons. . . . That is but a means to the ultimate end, which is the proper worship of God by all creatures."[9]

While *all* of life is to be worship, part of that life is to include gathering with other followers of Jesus for worship. This is the third sense of worship: corporate worship or *common worship*. Corporate or common worship has been a mark of the people of God since the time of the patriarchs in the Old Testament. After escaping from Egypt, the former Hebrew slaves received, via Moses, detailed instructions about the corporate worship of God. Jesus regularly joined his fellow Jews in worship in the synagogue on the Sabbath. The early Christians were told to avoid "neglecting to meet together, as is the habit of some" (Heb 10:25). This volume is chiefly concerned with this third circle of worship—corporate or common worship. We will be discussing the typical evangelical Protestant Sunday morning worship service—that is, the service of the word, without the celebration of the Lord's Supper. (The technical term for this is "antecommunion," literally "before Communion.")

The final and smallest circle of worship is that of the individual, the solitary Christian at worship. This is seen in the widespread practice of a daily "quiet time," often guided by one of a myriad of daily devotional books, or when a person slips quietly into a church sanctuary during the lunch break to pray, or into a college chapel between classes. For some it means praying daily the "offices" of the church, together with reading the lectionary-appointed Scripture lessons. For others, the practice of *Lectio Divina*[10] has proved to be an important tool for such private worship. Whatever the method or location, whenever an individual Christian privately engages in praise and thanksgiving, confession, the reading of Scripture, and response, then worship in this fourth sense is taking place.

Why Common Worship?

Countless pastors have despaired of people who tell them that they don't need corporate or common worship, that all they need or want is their own private devotional life. Innumerable reasons, it seems, are given for this conclusion:

"Some people who attend common worship are hypocritical" (True. But the church is for sinners, not the perfected, and chances are you're hypocritical sometimes, too.)

"The weekend is my only time off and I don't want to get up early on Sunday morning." (But do you have any trouble getting up early to take your daughter or son to early morning hockey practice, or getting up early for the start of vacation or the Boxing Day sales?)

"It's a big hassle because my children don't want to come." (They also don't want to go to school sometimes, abide by a curfew, or eat nutritious food instead of candy, and they give you a hassle about these things. So presumably they are illiterate, come and go whenever they please, and eat nothing but junk food?)

"You don't need the church to be a Christian." (True, but according to Scripture you *do* need the church and common worship if you intend to be an obedient Christian—a maturing, growing, learning Christian.)

The question of "why common worship?" is not merely academic. It is a real, ongoing issue affecting local churches, families, and individuals, an issue that deserves serious thought and attention.

Put in the simplest possible way, we should engage in common or corporate worship for two reasons: God commands (and deserves) it, and we need it.

God not only commands worship but also specifically commands common worship in Scripture. In the Hebrew Scriptures, the command is given repeatedly for the people of Israel to gather for worship. In addition to the constant worship services at the temple in Jerusalem, all adult males were commanded to journey to Jerusalem three times a year for worship during the great festivals of Passover, of Weeks, and of Booths (Exod 34:18-23; Deut 16:16). The psalm writers call people to common worship over and over: "O come, let *us* sing to the Lord; let *us* make a joyful noise to the rock of our salvation! Let *us* come into his presence with thanksgiving; let *us* make a joyful noise to him with songs of praise. . . . O come let *us* worship and bow down" (Ps 95:1-2, 6, emphasis added). In the New Testament, Jesus himself sets the example of common worship: "He went to the synagogue on the Sabbath day, as was his custom" (Luke 4:16). The book of Acts makes it clear that common worship was the norm in the early church. Indeed, at first it seems that common worship was a daily event (Acts 4:46-47)! It was simply assumed that regular worship gatherings would occur, modeled to a large degree on existing Jewish worship.

The biblical witness is not just that God commands that we worship, and specifically commands common worship, but also that he *deserves* our worship. This is why the psalm writers insist repeatedly that God's greatness deserves praise (for example, Pss 18:3; 48:1; 96:4; 145:3). God is worthy, sing the twenty-four elders in Revelation, "to receive glory and honor and power" (Rev 5:11).

For an evangelical who takes a high view of the authority of Scripture and is committed to God's lordship, God's command to gather in common worship, not to mention worship being affirmed by Scripture as something that is God's right and due, should be sufficient reasons to engage in common worship.

Saying only that God commands worship, particularly common worship, even saying this worship is his right and due, could suggest that God is egotistical, constantly needing to be praised and fawned over. The reality of course is that God does not need anything—including the common worship of his human creatures. God is holy, and the root of that word—holy—means to be separate, cut off, independent, self-sufficient. God is, in fact, altogether holy, altogether self-sufficient, and needs nothing. *It is not God who needs our worship but the other way around*—it is we who need to worship and in particular we who need to engage in common worship.

As creatures we were made—designed—in such a way that *we* need to worship. Not worshipping is abnormal and leads through emptiness and lack of meaning to spiritual death. Being truly and fully human requires that we worship. "Worship," as Hughes Oliphant Old wrote, "is at the centre of our existence, at the heart of our reason for being."[11] Furthermore, we were designed specifically to worship *together*, to engage in *common worship*. Is this not part of the deep meaning of the story of Adam and Eve—regardless of whether one understands this as literal or symbolic text (Gen 2:15–3:24)? Where once there had been only the possibility of solitary worship, now with two humans there is the possibility of common worship. But in choosing their way instead of God's, Adam and Eve are refusing to worship, specifically refusing to engage in common worship, rejecting an attitude of service, submission, reverential respect, and both recognition and acceptance of God's sovereignty or lordship. Tellingly, instead of *seeking* the face of God—one of the phrases the First Testament uses for worship—the two "hid themselves from the presence of the LORD God" (Gen 3:8). Without it, we will die.

It might even be argued that common worship is even *more* needful since the fall than before! A person who repents of sin and confesses Christ as Lord does not instantly become perfect, completely aligned with the will of God and fully obedient to God. Although saved, we remain fallen human beings, deeply twisted from God's purposes. Common worship is one of the chief means by which we are, albeit slowly, untwisted, a process that will not be completed until after death. As Leanne Van Dyk puts it,

> It is in worship that our lives are formed by the Holy Spirit and informed by God's Word. It is in worship that our theology is shaped, our discipleship encouraged, and our spirits fed by the good food of word and sacrament. It is from worship that we are sent out into the world to continue to live the patterns of life we have begun to learn and practice in worship.[12]

On a practical level, the reality is that without regular common worship, few will survive as followers of Christ. "If our people are going to live the Christ-like life," writes Kyle Childress, pastor of Austin Heights Baptist Church in Nacogdoches, Texas,

> then they had better do it as a body or else they'll never make it. Lone individuals trying to live faithfully cannot stand against sin, death, the Powers, and the overwhelming pressure of society. Both we and our people, as individuals, are easy pickings for the Powers of Death; they'll separate us, isolate us, dis-member us, pick us off one at a time and grind us down into the dust.[13]

In a secular society where neither the culture nor its institutions support faith any longer—Christian or otherwise—this need for common worship is especially pronounced.

The Purposes of Common Worship

We have tried to define common worship and understand why it is necessary. It seems natural that now we start thinking about the *purposes* of common worship. What is common worship supposed to accomplish or do? What are the goals or aims of common worship?

In one critical respect, this question—what is common worship supposed to do—is entirely wrongheaded. It assumes that common worship is intended to accomplish some "practical" goal, perhaps winning people to faith, allowing people to experience a sense of God's presence, motivating Christians to be more active in feeding the poor, or a host of other worthy things. But that simply is not worship as the Bible understands it. Nowhere does the Bible say that worship is to be undertaken so that some "practical" goal or other may be achieved. Simon Chan puts the biblical understanding of common worship succinctly: "*worship is never meant to serve any other purpose except the glory of God.* The end of worship is worship."[14] J. Daniel Day concurs. Day, formerly Senior Professor of Christian Preaching and Worship at Campbell University Divinity School, pastored Baptist churches in Texas, Louisiana, Missouri, and Oklahoma. He writes, "Worship is about God. It isn't about selling God . . . being inspired by God-referencing programs . . . 'experiencing' God. Worship is about God. Period."[15] Commenting on John's vision of heavenly worship in chapter 24 of the book of Revelation, Cornelius Plantinga, former President of Calvin Theological Seminary, and Sue Rozeboom, of Western Theological Seminary point out,

> *Everything* [emphasis added] they [the twenty-four elders] say and do says, *You, O living God, are worthy, and I am unworthy; you are great and I am small; you are God and I am not.* These elders acclaim God's high status. They call attention to God's excellent character. They declare God's mighty acts. God is not only powerful, having "created all things," but also gracious, having willed all things into existence.[16]

Using the picture of the four circles, we see that the purpose of common worship is to lead us to the larger circles of worship involving the totality of our day-to-day lives and ultimately joining ourselves with the worship of all creation.

The fact that so many evangelicals cannot think of common worship except in terms of it accomplishing some "practical" goal reveals that, when it comes to worship, our worldview is shaped not by Scripture but by our culture. From the perspective of a secular society in which God has been shuffled to the attic rooms, the edges of life, worshipping God simply for the sake of the worship of God comes across as a waste of time, energy, and resources. Worship doesn't "do" anything. To such a secular mindset, God and the worship of God quite clearly are not central. Such worship appears to be a royal waste of time, as Marva Dawn wonderfully titled one of her books.[17] But from the biblical perspective, which always sees God as the centre, the eternal worship of God is the ultimate goal for *all* creation. Worship is the heart of what it means to be truly human. Worship is the act of a creature in right relationship with the Creator. For the church—the people who confess the Lordship of Christ, in and through whom we have come to know God best—common worship should be at our centre as we press toward the goal of being more and more fully in right relationship with God.

Simply put, the primary work of the entire creation, the church, and individuals is worship. Period. Full stop. This is a difficult idea for many of us who grew up in the evangelical world. Robert Webber, who devoted much of his career to thinking and writing about worship is not unusual in his experience:

> For as long as I can remember, it was impressed upon me that the most important part of being a Christian was being a witness. . . . I was told . . . that my single calling in life was to be a soul winner. . . . Evangelism is an exceedingly important work of the church . . . . But it is worship . . . that really stands behind all these activities. The church is first a worshipping community. Evangelism and other functions of ministry flow from the worship of the church.[18]

Our understanding of worship has been distorted by the secular culture in which we live. We think worship must serve some purpose other than worship. It does not. Moreover, in thinking this way we unwittingly shift the focus of our common worship from God to a host of other goals. Most of these other goals are laudable, but they are not God. And the moment the focus of worship shifts from the worship of God, the moment God is even slightly sidelined, that worship has started to be secularized, for something other than God is now central—which is of course what secularization means.

The By-products of Common Worship

When common worship is actually focused on its one true purpose or goal—the worship of God—*out of such worship* come a variety of important and beneficial "by-products." In this instance, the term "by-product" means something valuable that is created, secondary to the creation of something else. For instance, a lumber mill produces lumber with which to construct buildings. Two by-products of what the mill creates are sawdust and shavings. These can be used for a variety of purposes, from animal bedding and gardening mulch to pellets for wood-burning stoves. The sawdust and shavings are good, useful, and beneficial, but without the goal of producing the lumber, they would not be created.

The same principle applies to worship in general and common worship in particular. When the focus is on God and the one true goal of worshipping God simply for the sake of worshipping God, certain important "by-products" are created. If somehow the focus on worship's true goal is forgotten, misunderstood, or abandoned, the by-products will not be created at all or will be created in distorted ways. That this is the case should not come as a surprise. An important theme of the teaching of Jesus was that the only way to gain life, paradoxically, was to give it up (Matt 6:25; 16:25; Mark 8:35; Luke 9:24; 17:33). If one tries to hold on to life tightly, hoarding it to oneself, one finally has no life, now or eternally. Trying desperately to hold on to life makes it not bigger but smaller, lesser and poorer. This is the way things work in the divine economy. So also with worship. Trying to create, obtain, or hold on to the beneficial by-products that stem from genuine worship is the one sure way to miss out on them. Only by giving ourselves up completely to worship—worship that has as its goal simply and solely the worship and praise of God—can we obtain the by-products. "If," as Christopher Ellis, former principal of Bristol Baptist College in England, puts it,

> we set out to worship in order to gain various benefits, then we are putting ourselves at the centre of our concern, rather than God, and so are not truly worshipping God. [It is] . . . treating worship as a means to an end . . . . This is self-defeating because those benefits do not accrue unless we are truly worshipping God. . . . This is God's economy—the way things work in the kingdom—put God first, and his kingdom and all the rest will be added to you (Matthew 6:33).[19]

Those who have responsibility for the planning of any aspect of a worship service or give leadership in such a service need constantly to be evaluating, first, whether the service is focused on the worship of God for the sake of the worship of God and, second, whether these by-products are clearly being created. If they are not, then the painful question must be asked whether the focus and goal really has been on God and his worship.

With this absolutely critical understanding in place, we can ask, what are the by-products of common worship that is focused entirely on the worship of God—and nothing else?

One helpful way of understanding the "by-products" of worship is to categorize them under eight headings: Formation, Meaning, Counterculture, Community, Experience of God's Presence, Encouragement, Salt and Light, Response of Kingdom Work.

Formation

We have all heard the old saying, "You are what you eat." From the perspective of Scripture, a much more important truth is "You are what you worship" or, more precisely, "You come to resemble what you worship." N. T. Wright summarizes this extremely well:

> When you gaze in awe, admiration, and wonder at something or someone, you begin to take on something of the character of the object of your worship. Those who worship money become, eventually, human calculating machines. Those who worship sex become obsessed with their own attractiveness or prowess. Those who worship power become more and more ruthless.[20]

Both the Old and New Testaments are adamant that worship *forms*—changes—the worshipper. When the first humans accept the worthiness of the serpent and his advice, they are changed. They are formed into something *less*, rather than more, like God. On the edge of entering the promised land, the people of God are warned that they should not even ask about the loathsome worship practices of the previous inhabitants of the land, lest they be tempted to adopt such practices (Deut 12:29-32) and presumably become similarly loathsome. The book of 2 Kings laments that the people "went after false idols, and became false" (2 Kings 17:15). In Jeremiah, God declares that the people of Israel "went after worthless things and became worthless" (Jer 2:4). Paul, in his letter to the Romans, insists that failure to worship the one true God results in people becoming "futile in their thinking," "senseless," and "fools" (Rom 1:21-22). The point is obvious, isn't it? *All* worship changes or forms the worshipper—for good or ill.

From the biblical perspective, formation in the positive sense means the process of being transformed or changed, so that increasingly a person is like the God who has been revealed to us most clearly in Jesus. Hence, Paul, addressing the churches of Galatia wrote, "I am again in the pain of childbirth until Christ is formed in you" (Gal 4:19). Being like Jesus means being fully attuned to and obedient to the will of God. Being like Jesus also means that I will increasingly reflect and mimic the inner life of the very Trinity itself, of which Jesus is a part. That inner life, or centre of God, is a mutual, self-sacrificing love. At the very centre of God's existence is the desire to serve rather than be served, lovingly, joyfully, and without any sense of coercion to sacrifice for and submit to the other.

This kind of formation is one of the by-products of worship that is focused solely on the worship of God for the sake of the worship of God. Not of course that common worship is the *only* means by which such transformation takes place. There are many other tools at our disposal, ranging from being part of a local church, private devotions, journaling, and online Bible studies to involvement in spiritual retreats, church camps, and small accountability or study groups, not to mention learning to love others and to serve them in practical ways. But common worship is one of the most important means of transformation—"tools"—we have been given to bring about this kind of change.

Why is it that common worship can help us in the process of being formed in the likeness of Jesus? In common worship we acknowledge and submit ourselves to the lordship of God, whom we know best in Jesus, God come among us. In common worship we give up control, trying to do things our way. Ben Witherington III writes, "Worship . . . is where the creature recognizes that he or she is a creature and God alone is the Creator. Worship is an act of submission, of placing oneself under the deity. This of course, also implies a denial . . . that one is lord over one's own life."[21] The hope is that each time I join with others in common worship, a small piece of "me"—the false "me" that insists on having its own way over against God—dies and is replaced by a true "me" that is subject to God's will. The hope is that eventually there will be nothing left of the false "me." Only the true and fully human "me" that is joyfully obedient to God will remain. This is surely what Paul meant when he wrote, "it is no longer I who live, but it is Christ who lives in me" (Gal 2:20).

This process of formation—becoming more and more like Jesus—is neither simple nor easy, and it is particularly difficult in the context of a secular society. Make no mistake about it: Christians—that is, those who are consciously committed to the Lordship of Christ, genuinely dedicated to becoming more and more like him—are a small minority in Western society, which is now primarily secular in nature. Western society was once a place in which matters of faith, specifically Christian faith, dominated both the public square and private discourse. That is no longer the case. Let's be clear: for individuals, a secular approach to life *does not* mean people no longer believe that God exists. Atheism is *not* the problem. In fact, most Canadians, Americans, and Western Europeans do believe that God, or a "higher power" of some sort, exists. Indeed many also affirm a pastiche of frequently contradictory views, many more or less recognizably Christian in nature. But these beliefs simply do not form, shape, or direct day-to-day life. A secular person does not consider such beliefs when deciding what career path to choose, what sexual behaviour to engage in, what business practices in which to engage, or what political party to support. At the societal, public square level, where once great questions were debated from an explicitly Christian perspective, today it is highly unusual for an issue of public policy—be that the social safety net, military spending, or foreign policy—to be discussed on a faith basis.

We are constantly immersed in this secular approach to life. There is no way to escape it short of becoming a hermit living in some remote place. Marva Dawn for example argues that our worldview is shaped to a large extent by the twenty-eight hours or so that the average person watches TV weekly, which gives the message, "You are the most important thing on the face of the earth. Your immediate desires are all that count. Do It Your Way."[22] J. Daniel Day points out,

> those who wish to become Christian in any age must be detoxified from the world's "mind" and . . . molded into a distinctively new, Christly culture. In this re-formation corporate worship plays a crucial role . . . . the world's culture is so pervasive and toxic that its fatal fumes are inhaled unwittingly. From this we desperately need "saving . . . ." This change will not come in a moment, but surely the discipline of worship ought to have a role to play in . . . weaning us from this culture of death and introducing us to a redemptive culture of Christ-life."[23]

Constantly being immersed in and surrounded by a secular approach to life, and being a minority within this culture, those who are followers of Jesus discover that common worship is absolutely essential. When we join with others in praising God, we are affirming, over against our culture, that God alone—not the latest celebrity or politician or supermarket product or political product—is worthy of ultimate praise. Similarly, "when we give thanks to God in worship, we are not only thanking him for this or that, we are learning to view the world with gratitude and to see and experience life as a gift."[24] Instead of complaining about our not being able to afford the most recent electronic gadget, we are learning to be grateful for the plethora of things we have, which we regularly take for granted. Regular involvement in common worship forces us to see—and confess—those places where our thinking and actions are not conformed to the likeness of Jesus, where we have instead accepted the values, attitudes, and ideas of the secular ethos that surrounds us. In common worship, particularly as a result of sound preaching, we will find ourselves asking how everything from our work, our family lives, and the way we vote to where and how we shop are or aren't aligning with our profession of Christ as Lord. Common worship regularly reminds worshippers that they are supposed to be different from secular people. Common worship challenges us to live differently, in obedience to Christ, and it teaches us what that means. It educates us to think theologically and critically so that we may avoid—to paraphrase the famous paraphrase of Romans 12:2 by J. B. Phillips—being squeezed into the mold of the secular world in which we live.[25] In common worship "our lives, purpose, identities, and hopes [are] conformed to that 'new world' into which the Word and Spirit give us new birth—instead of the other way around."[26] Common worship leads to response. Together we "pray for the world [and in so doing] we are also forming certain attitudes in ourselves, feeling for the world as we believe God feels for the world, and that will make a difference in our actions."[27] This response means that "[w]hen we leave [common] worship we . . . field test the things we have learned."[28]

Genuine common worship, when engaged in seriously and regularly, "creates a great impact on the hearts and minds and lives of a congregation's members."[29] That this is so should hardly come as a surprise. Over and over in the Bible, when people meet with God they are changed in some way. Emil Brunner pointed out repeatedly that in the biblical sense, truth is not so much a set of facts as it is an encounter with God, who is the ultimate truth, and that encounter inevitably changes the one who encounters

God.[30] If common worship entails meeting with God regularly, we will inevitably be changed, transformed. It cannot be otherwise.

Meaning

The formation that flows from common worship is formation according to what is really real, formation according to the deepest, most basic, most central reality of all. Such worship, founded on deepest reality, cannot help but impart real meaning to human life. Common worship provides this meaning by situating each of us and all of creation within a "grand narrative" that has God as both its origin and consummation.

Of course the very idea of any kind of "metanarrative," that is, any kind of comprehensive explanation of things, is anathema to postmodern thought. Postmodernists insist that all we can have are countless individual explanations of reality. There is no possibility of any great story, a grand narrative, an absolute truth that orders and explains reality, knowledge, and experience. Ironically, the postmodern insistence that there is no metanarrative is itself a metanarrative! For postmodernists, the various ways people see the world are subjective and often distorted by power structures that create these differing viewpoints. In the end, therefore, whatever anyone says about anything is merely that person's subjective "opinion."

Postmodernism is in many respects a much-needed corrective to some of the excesses of Enlightenment (i.e., modern) thought. Much of Enlightenment thinking assumed not only that fallen human reason was capable of completely objective thought but also that human senses, employing the empirical method, were the only means of ascertaining truth. (Reality, in other words, consisted solely of things that could be touched, tasted, heard, smelled, or seen, and human senses were adequate to identify and understand these things.)

The biblical witness finds fault with *both* modern and postmodern approaches. In contradiction to modern thought, Scripture takes the position that there is a reality beyond the one that mere human sensory functions can ascertain. Further, Scripture is very realistic in seeing human reason as flawed and imperfect. On the other hand, the biblical witness also rejects the notion that there is no grand story. While the Bible says human beings need to be extremely humble about their ability to understand that story and where they fit into it, it has no doubt that there is such a story.

Scripture says that we find our meaning and purpose only when we worship, only when we find our place in that fourth and ultimate circle of worship—the worship of the Creator by all creation. *That* is the story. That is what we were created for, how we were designed, and outside of that we miss our purpose and lack meaning. Anything other than worship as our ultimate purpose is inadequate to provide our lives with purpose. Common worship, the worship of the church, leads us toward and joins us with that great story, the never-ending cosmic hymn of praise.

By definition, a secular worldview, whether influenced by modern or postmodern thought, cannot define or draw meaning for life from God or the worship of God. Instead, human beings must struggle to create and sustain meaning from their relationships, work, causes, leisure pursuits, and accomplishments—from their own stories among a plethora of stories. All of these things may indeed provide some meaning to life, but none of them can give any permanent sense of meaning. Is it any wonder then that so many in our culture are bored and world weary, often at a very young age? Why bother? Nothing matters! What point is there to it all? "Secularization says that all that is, is what is. It argues that there is nothing outside of human existence to give life meaning or value."[31]

In glaring contrast, "worship stands in opposition to the secular trend that repudiates the supernatural . . . . it reaffirms the reality of God, the significance of life, and the worth of the human person."[32] Christian worship affirms that God intends to remake and restore his creation, that every good thing in creation will find its place in that renewed creation. Nothing good will be lost. As N. T. Wright puts it,

> You are not oiling the wheels of a machine that's about to roll over a cliff. You are not restoring a great painting that's shortly going to be thrown on the fire. You are not planting roses in a garden that's about to be dug up for a building site. You are—strange though it may seem, almost as hard to believe as the resurrection itself—accomplishing something that will become in due course part of God's new world. Every act of love, gratitude, and kindness; every work of art or music inspired by the love of God and delight in the beauty of his creation . . . every act of care and nurture, of comfort and support, for one's fellow human beings and for that matter one's fellow nonhuman creatures; and of course every prayer, all Spirit-led teaching, every deed that spreads the gospel, builds up the church, embraces and embodies holiness rather than corruption, and makes the name of Jesus honoured in the world—all of this will find its way, through the resurrecting power of God, into the new creation that God will one day make.[33]

Common worship affirms that humans are *not* merely random collections of atoms in the midst of a cold, uncaring blob of a universe that has given us consciousness that only allows us to realize we have no purpose. By leading us toward and connecting us with the worship of all creation, common worship constantly shows us that there *is* a point to our lives, there *is* meaning, and affirms that God alone is the source of all true and enduring meaning.

Countercultural

Worship that affirms that we find meaning in God's service and God's worship alone is, by its very nature, countercultural. Such worship challenges all other supposed sources of meaning (or in the case of postmodernism, multiple meanings or non-meaning), all other "grand stories," and names them as worthless idols.

Throughout the Bible the descriptions and images of the people of God are always those of a minority, frequently a very small minority, compared to the wider population of those who do not accept God's sovereignty or lordship. Noah and his family alone honoured Yahweh, and Abraham was called out from his country and clan. Hebrews describes Abraham, Isaac, and Jacob as "strangers and foreigners on the earth" (Heb 11:13). When in ancient times God's people took the form of an actual nation-state, Israel, that nation was never more than a small entity compared to many of its neighbours. At the time of the Babylonian invasion of Judah, the concern of the exiles was how they could maintain their faith surrounded by those who, while not especially hostile to that faith, largely knew and cared little about it. How could they "sing the LORD's song in a strange land?" (Ps 137:4, AV) Canadian theologian Douglas John Hall has pointed out that the pictures of the church that Jesus gave were always those of a minority group within the wider civil community. The followers of Jesus were to be as salt (small in quantity compared to the amount of food), light (which in the ancient Middle East meant the modest oil lamp of a village home), yeast (a tiny portion of a loaf of bread), or a mustard seed (a very small seed).[34] Throughout the book of Acts, local churches are consistently pictured as small gatherings proportionate to the wider community. Peter's first letter refers to Christians as "aliens and exiles" (1 Pet 2:11). In Greek, the words used refer respectively to someone who lives in a place other than his own country, an expatriate, and to a person who is staying for a while in a strange place.

It was only with the "Constantinian settlement"—which first made Christianity legal within the Roman Empire, then favoured it, and finally made it the only permitted faith—that notions of the church being largely identical in membership with the wider civil society appeared. For well over a thousand years, this pattern held sway in Western Europe. Church and state were closely intertwined, with the church often acting virtually as another department of the government.

Given the biblical witness, it is passing strange that so many evangelical Christians, committed to a high view of the authority of Scripture, fail to see the church as being a countercultural minority within the wider civil society. Instead, particularly in North America (much less so in Western Europe), many evangelicals speak of wanting to create a "Christian country" or, more often, reestablishing such from a supposedly lost golden era. They fail to see any significant difference between the teachings of Jesus, the biblical description of the church in the New Testament as a profoundly countercultural minority, and the worldview of Western society. The result is that many evangelicals are seriously compromised, unable and unwilling to see the stark contrasts between the teachings of Jesus and the worldview, values, and economic and foreign policies of the nations of the Western world. Being unable to see these contradictions also means seeing no need to challenge or confront views, attitudes, and practices that clearly are opposite to the Kingdom priorities and ethics espoused by Jesus.

There is hope, however, despite our often being so compromised, and part of that hope is in common worship. Common worship that is truly focused on God and his worship simply for the sake of God and his worship has the power to turn worshippers into the kind of countercultural minority that the Bible consistently sees as the role of God's people. This kind of worship can expose the idols of our culture that claim to provide meaning. It has happened before, and it can happen again.

The ancient Jewish people almost invariably found themselves in one of two situations. Either they were living as a minority inside another nation (the pre-exodus Jews in Egypt, those exiled to Babylon after the fall of Jerusalem) or as residents of the nation-state of Israel, surrounded by other, larger, influential, powerful empires (Egypt, Assyria, Babylon, Persia). In a superb essay titled "Always in the Shadow of Empire," Walter Brueggemann notes that, often living in the shadow of some great power, Israel's common worship encouraged the community "to affirm *that the world constructed in liturgy* is more reliable and more credible than the world 'out there.' The purpose of such liturgy [was] to equip Israel with the nerve to act out of its distinctiveness in the face of formidable, hostile powers"[35]

Israel's constant temptation was to buy into the picture of reality set forth by the successive dominant powers of the day and their religions—Egypt, Assyria, Babylon, Persia. The detailed instructions given by God concerning Israel's worship both in the desert and in the temple in Jerusalem, and the insistence on Sabbath observance, were clearly intended to keep Israel and Israel's faith in Yahweh separate and apart from the surrounding religions and their practices. Israel's worship constantly set out a different, countercultural depiction of reality. Of course, few if any in modern Western society are tempted to adopt the worldviews of the superpowers of the ancient Middle East! That does not, however, mean that our culture has no powerful rival pictures of reality to that given in Scripture. In contemporary Western society, the dominant alternative is espoused by secular people, "those for whom Yahweh has dropped out of the narrative of the world."[36]

Similarly for the early church, common worship was about distinguishing the followers of Jesus from the followers of the multitude of other worldviews that flourished in the Roman Empire. Many of the church's earliest controversies and debates, such as those about circumcision and eating meat sacrificed to idols, were really about how to maintain distinctiveness. Likewise, much of the preaching in the New Testament church focused on the insistence that, contrary to the official position of the empire, Jesus, not the emperor, was Lord, that Jesus as Lord was the true and accurate depiction of reality, as opposed to the official political "line" of Imperial Rome.

One of the by-products in our time of genuine common worship—worship focused on God—should be that such worship consistently contradicts the dominant secular picture of reality in our society and makes more real the biblical picture of reality. For Christians in contemporary Western society, the dominant picture is of a world in which God simply doesn't matter and isn't important, a world from which God is largely absent. Genuine common worship should create followers of Jesus Christ who are aware they are a minority within the wider culture, understand what the differences are between Christianity and Western culture, and are equipped to challenge the dominant, secular worldview. "True worship," as Stuart Murray, chair of the *UK Anabaptist Network* writes, "is profoundly counter-cultural, calling worshippers to embrace an alternative vision, deviant values and a different metanarrative."[37] Such "worship will convey the framework of faith in which everything is to be understood."[38] A framework, need one add, in which God is not only not absent or unimportant but the most important player. "If the Church's worship is faithful, it will . . . transform the lives of those nurtured by it. Worship will turn our values, habits, and ideas upside-down as it forms our character: only then will we be genuinely right-side up eternally." It is hard to imagine that worship in which "The Lordship of Jesus Christ [is] the presiding conviction"[39] could do otherwise!

The pointed questions that we evangelicals need to ask ourselves include: Does our common worship, Sunday by Sunday, actually contradict the dominant, secular worldview? If so, how? Does it do so consciously and consistently? Does our common worship set out the alternate picture of reality given in Scripture? Does it "train [us] to see reality in a thoroughly different way" from that of a secular culture?[40] Does common worship affirm that my primary identity is not my gender, marital status, job (or lack thereof), level of education, the size of my home, or the nationality identified in my passport but rather my status as a child of God, a redeemed follower of Jesus Christ whom I confess as Lord? Does common worship challenge what John Jefferson Davis argues are the two major competing worldviews of Western society that stem from the Enlightenment—modernism and postmodernism?[41] The former, in its atheistic form, sees matter as all there is and has no place at all for God or, in its softer, deistic form, allows for the existence of God but sees God as distant and uninvolved in life, thus disallowing the possibility of miracles. Postmodernism, on the other hand, in some respects a reaction to the overweening emphasis on human reason in modernism, says that every worldview is merely a social construct, usually of a dominant and oppressive group, and denies that there is any possibility of having an overarching story for life.[42] For postmodernism, there is no possibility of truth or final reality. Both worldviews contribute significantly to a secular approach to daily life.

If we are honest, do we have to admit that much evangelical worship actually supports and even fosters a secular approach to life? If the focus and purpose of worship are other than God and worshipping God for the sake of worshipping God, then such worship, having nudged God to some place other than the centre, has itself become secularized. Inevitably, such worship will not be, indeed cannot be, countercultural.

Community

A critical by-product of common worship is maintaining community. Human beings were created to be in community. This should hardly be a surprise given that God is a community of three persons, whom we are meant to reflect. The absence or failure of community, be that community a marriage, a neighbourhood, or the community of humanity as a whole, is evidence of human sin. Even among the people of God, maintaining community has been a constant challenge.

The nation of Israel, and later the nations of Israel and Judah, frequently gave in to the temptation to adopt the practices, attitudes, economic systems, and gods of surrounding nations. Much of the prophetic literature roundly denounces these failures and warns of coming divine judgement. After Israel is invaded and disappears from history, its people largely assimilated, Judah continues a perilous existence for some time. But it too is eventually invaded, Jerusalem is laid waste, and many are exiled to Babylon. Surrounded by a culture that was usually indifferent to their faith, the exiles constantly faced the danger of assimilation. Consistently gathering for common worship was an important tool to resist that assimilation. In the early decades of the church's history, becoming a Christian not infrequently meant the loss of family, economic or social connections, networks, and support systems. One's fellow followers of Jesus became the new family and support system. Christians, a minority within secular Western society today, face the same challenges—and have the same tool of common worship available to them.

Common worship, as it was for exiles then, is also for exiles now a means to create and maintain community. Such worship affirms that "we" are not the same as "them." Week by week, month by month, year by year, as the followers of Jesus gather from across a district, town, or city, we see the distinct community of the church made visible. We are encouraged by being reminded that we are not alone in this countercultural endeavour. In common worship, especially in preaching, we are, hopefully, reminded not only that there are boundaries between the church and secular society but also what those boundaries are and how to discern them. The church becomes more than a collection of like-minded individuals; it becomes a support system and a new family, a genuine and deep community.

Experience of God's Presence

There is no question that the individual believer engaged in private worship may have genuine and powerful affective experiences of God's presence.

There are countless examples of this to be found in both Testaments and in the church's subsequent history. Equally both the first and second Testaments and the history of the church demonstrate that in common worship, people may powerfully experience God's presence.

When Jesus said, "where two or three are gathered in my name, I am there among them" (Matt 18:20), he surely did not mean he would not be present with the individual Christian at his or her prayers! But he must have meant *something*. That *something* would seem to be that God is more powerfully experienced, or at least differently experienced, when Christians worship together than when they worship individually.

Paul described the church as the body of Christ of which each individual Christian forms a part (1 Cor 12:12-27). According to the apostle, the lone Christian is incomplete without the rest of the church. The notion of the lone Christian is about as sensible as the concept of a body made up only of an eye or an ear. Does it not follow then that private, individual worship by itself misses something? Just as no one organ or body part can experience the full range of senses, so also it would seem that no one Christian, on his or her own, can experience the full range of God's presence that is possible in common worship.

Encouragement

Encouragement is another of the by-products of worship that is simply for the sake of worship. The very act of meeting regularly with others who also gather for the purpose of worshipping God for the sake of the worship of God is an important reminder that I am not in this alone. I am not the only one who is being formed to look like Jesus, not the only one who finds genuine meaning only in the worship and service of God, not the only one who is swimming against the cultural stream, not the only one who senses God's presence in worship.

In a secular society, it is far from easy to be a follower of Jesus Christ, where that is a distinctly minority and countercultural choice. The woman or man who is truly serious about following Christ will often be alone in that commitment in the office or shop, on the sports team, or in the classroom. It is not even uncommon to be the only such person in one's family. It is never easy to maintain a commitment alone, to be the voice crying in the wilderness. The first Christians, also a countercultural minority, struggled with the same difficulties. Like Christians today, they too needed others who provided encouragement to keep on keeping on, and who could give useful advice about how to do so. Hence, in an account of the worship of the church in Antioch, Judas and Silas "said much to encourage and strengthen the believers" (Acts 15:32). Hebrews connects "meeting together" with "encouraging one another" (Heb 10:25).

Individual and common worship could be seen as comparable to many sports. In the congregation I currently serve, several people are marathoners. Much of the time, training for a marathon is a solitary pursuit, but from time to time, groups of runners come together for practice meets. In addition to being reminded that there are others sharing the same passion—despite the fact that friends and family may consider it very strange to run long distances, sometimes in extreme temperatures, for pleasure—this is an opportunity to exchange ideas and strategies about what works well and what doesn't work at all. The purpose of such meets is running—not conversation or advice about the best or latest equipment, orthopedics, or avoiding inattentive drivers. But out of the meet focused on running come important by-products.

Salt and Light

In the Sermon on the Mount, Jesus described the characteristics of a Kingdom person, in other words, what one of his followers should look like. Among other things, his followers are described as "salt" and "light" (Matt 5:13-14).

In the ancient world, one of the chief uses of salt was as a preservative. Salt kept stored food from rotting. In some mysterious fashion, the very existence of Christians keeps the world from being as rotten and corrupt as it would be otherwise. Recall for a moment the discussion of the four circles of worship. Only when creatures find their place in the largest circle—the never-ending anthem of the universe—do they find fulfillment and joy. Only when all creation is part of that anthem will the universe be set to rights again. All the other circles of worship—including common worship—are intended to join us to this biggest circle of worship. That means that *every* time Christians gather in common worship, something extraordinary is happening: the wider world is being held back from further alienation from God, being nudged back toward God. *Every* service of common worship is, in some mysterious fashion, recovering and reestablishing God's intention for creation.

Light, of course, shows things the way they really are. As the true light, Jesus changes and makes realistic how we see ourselves, others, the wider creation, and God. Followers of Christ are supposed to show to the world the reality that life lived apart from the recognition of God's lordship is unfulfilling, lacking in meaning and deep joy, and, in the end, deadly. Common worship that is intended to be central to our lives as Christians cannot help but show forth this reality.

As Marva J. Dawn explains, [Simply] "By offering worship that educates instead of entertains, that uplifts and transforms through the renewing of the mind (Rom. 12:2), the Church exposes the meaninglessness of our present culture."[43] On the positive side, such worship constantly sets out the alternative (and true) picture of reality that we find in Scripture.

Response of Kingdom Work

It is critical to be absolutely clear on this point—what happens in the corporate gathering for common worship must *never* be divorced from the rest of life. If that happens, it is seriously questionable whether there was genuine common worship at all; at the very least it means that life has become secularized, leaving only the hour or two of weekly common worship under the reign of God.

Common worship that is focused on the worship of God for the sake of the worship of God will equip God's people for the coming week. Such worship trains us to look at all of life through the lens of worship, to think and act theologically as we move through the work and play, joys and sorrows, accomplishments and defeats of the week. But genuine common worship *also* leads to response, actually to doing Kingdom work.

The Kingdom of God was the central theme of the preaching of Jesus. He gave the clearest definition of the Kingdom in the model prayer he taught to his disciples. There he taught them to pray "thy kingdom come, thy will be done . . ." (Matt 6:10, AV). In typical fashion of the time, the second phrase explains or elaborates the meaning of the first. The Kingdom then is whenever and wherever the will of God is accomplished, his reign or rule realized. A by-product of genuine common worship is response in the form of doing Kingdom work. Evangelicals rightly insist on the Protestant Reformation's teaching that salvation is through grace accepted by faith, not works, *but* also that genuine faith is evidenced by good works. We similarly need to insist that genuine common worship is evidenced by real response—Kingdom work response.

Response as a by-product of common worship is the pattern we see over and over again in both Testaments. After God has revealed his commandments to Moses, he, Aaron, Nadam, Abihu, and seventy of the elders of Israel worship God. Moses then relays to the people the words God has spoken. And then? ". . . all the people answered with one voice, and said,

'All the words that the LORD has spoken we will do'" (Exod 24:3). The response in this instance is the people of God solemnly promising to obey God. When Solomon has completed building the temple, a great crowd gathers for common worship. The ark is placed in the temple, God's glory fills the place, and Solomon praises God and then prays a prayer that has elements of praise, thanksgiving, confession, and petition. Then both king and people respond with enormous numbers of sacrificial offerings and a great festival (1 Kings 8). After Nehemiah returns to Jerusalem to begin rebuilding, the people are gathered for worship. Ezra, the priest, retrieves the "book of the law"—presumably meaning the Torah, the first five books of the Bible. As soon as he opens the book, the people stand. Ezra praises God. The people lift up their hands, bow their heads to the ground, and worship God. Ezra reads—at great length—and others interpret or explain what is read (Neh 8:1-8). And then what happens? Response! First there is grief and weeping (8:9). It seems this was because the people realized how far they were from observing God's commandments. Second, there is rejoicing and feasting among the people (8:10-12), "because they had understood the words that were declared to them" (8:12). Third, the response continues the next day. Leaders of the people gather for further study of Scripture; they discover what is taught about observing the festival of booths and reinstitute its observance (8:13-18). Fourth, the response is not just for one or two days. The response to this common worship continues for weeks afterward! Nehemiah records another service of worship in which the people spend a quarter of the day reading from Scripture and another quarter confessing their sins and worshipping (9:1-3)! Ezra leads in a long prayer to God that recalls the history of God's dealings with his people across the centuries, and the people and their leaders make a solemn oath before God (9:6–10:40) and take immediate action to arrange for the care of the temple (11–12).

In the New Testament the pattern is seen again—a by-product of common worship is some kind of response that is about seeing God's will, the Kingdom, realized. After the extraordinary events on the day of Pentecost, the followers of Jesus are described in this way: "They devoted themselves to the apostles' teaching and fellowship, to the breaking of bread and the prayers" (Acts 2:42). This can conceivably be read as a description of the overall work and ministry of the church, a description of common worship among the first Christians, or both. If we assume that in those early days there was little or no distinction between common worship and worship in the context of day-to-day life (the second and third circles of worship), then what follows this passage must surely be seen as response stemming from common worship. In this instance, that response included communal sharing of property (Acts 2:44-45). At first, many of the Christians continued to worship in the synagogues as they had always done. When this later became impossible, as those who regarded Jesus as the Messiah were barred from worship in the synagogue, much of the pattern of synagogue worship was simply carried over to gatherings for explicitly Christian worship. That synagogue pattern included prayers and readings followed by exposition of Scripture. After a benediction came a response in the form of a collection for the poor. It seems clear that this same pattern of worship/response is being described by Paul in his first letter to the Corinthians. There he gives instructions—the same as he had already given to the churches in Galatia—that on the first day of the week, the day of Christian worship, each person was to set aside money that would be taken to Jerusalem to relieve the poor Christians in that place (1 Cor 16:1-2). It takes little to assume that this collection would be received when the believers in Corinth gathered for common worship on the Lord's Day. Here is the church, responding to common worship, acting to see God's will, the Kingdom, realized—that the poor be fed. John, in his revelation, describes worship in heaven itself—and there too common worship ends with response. In this instance the response consists of throwing down crowns: "whenever the living creatures give glory, honor and thanks to the one who is seated on the throne . . . the twenty-four elders fall before the one who is seated on the throne and worship the one who lives forever and ever; they cast their crowns before the throne" (Rev 4:9-10).

While the form the response takes may vary enormously—from repentance to motivation for deeper study of Scripture, from communal sharing of property to acting to assist the poor—that there will be response as a by-product of genuine common worship should not be in doubt. Neither can there be any doubt that this response should get outside the walls of the church building into the wider world. Surely the Jesus who taught that everyone in need is our neighbour does not intend that our response to him will stop at the doors of a church building! As Marva Dawn puts it,

> Genuine worship of God will send us out for the sake of the neighbor. We cannot ascribe to the Lord the glory of his name (that is, his character) without imitating him in lavishly establishing justice and peace in the world. We cannot keep our generous God as our . . . Center without wanting our neighbours to be immersed in his opulent splendour, too.[44]

Genuine common worship will inevitably send us out into our society like the first evangelicals, who were determined to change their world for Christ. We will find ourselves compelled to witness and to engage in missions. We will engage more deeply with and challenge aspects of our culture that stand in opposition to Kingdom values, and we will find ourselves advocating and working for social justice, change, and reform. J. Daniel Day summarizes, "From this encounter with her Lord that we call worship *all* [emphasis added] the rest of the Church's ministries flow."[45]

Notes

1. C. F. D. Moule, *Worship in the New Testament*, Ecumenical Studies in Worship, ed. J. G. Davies and A. Raymond George (London: Lutterworth, 1967) 84.

2. Ibid., 85.

3. John Jefferson Davis, *Worship and the Reality of God: An Evangelical Theology of Real Presence* (Downers Grove IL: InterVarsity Press, 2010) 10.

4. Christopher J. Ellis, *Approaching God: A Guide for Worship Leaders and Worshippers* (Norwich: Canterbury Press, 2009) 3.

5. David Peterson, *Engaging with God: A Biblical Theology of Worship* (Downers Grove IL: InterVarsity Press, 1992) 18.

6. Ibid. 29.

7. Ben Witherington III, *We Have Seen His Glory: A Vision of Kingdom Worship*, Calvin Institute of Christian Worship Liturgical Studies Series, ed. John D. Witvliet (Grand Rapids MI: Eerdmans, 2010) 151.

8. Ibid., 7.

9. Ibid., 18.

10. *Lectio Divina* ("Holy Reading") is a method of scriptural reading, meditation, and prayer intended to promote communion with God and greater understanding of Scripture. The intention is not so much to study the text of Scripture critically as to reflect on and be open to what God is saying, presently, through a particular text. Although often thought of as a traditional Roman Catholic practice, *Lectio Divina* in fact existed well before the division of Western Christianity into Protestantism and Roman Catholicism. In recent years the practice has also been adopted by some evangelical Protestants.

11. Hughes Oliphant Old, *Worship: Reformed According to Scripture*, revised and expanded (Louisville: Westminster John Knox Press, 2002) 1.

12. Leanne Van Dyk, introduction to *A More Profound Alleluia: Theology and Worship in Harmony*, ed. Leanne Van Dyk, Calvin Institute of Christian Worship Liturgical Studies Series, ed. John D. Witvliet (Grand Rapids MI: Eerdmans, 2005) xv.

13. Kyle Childress, "Worship and Becoming the Body of Christ," in *Gathering Together: Baptists at Work in Worship*, ed. Rodney Wallace Kennedy, Derek C. Hatch (Eugene OR: Wipf and Stock, 2013) 5.

14. Simon Chan, *Liturgical Theology: The Church as Worshiping Community* (Downers Grove IL: InterVarsity Press, 2006) 53.

15. J. Daniel Day, *Seeking the Face of God: Evangelical Worship Reconceived* (Macon GA: Nurturing Faith, 2013) vii.

16. Cornelius Plantinga Jr. and Sue Rozeboom, *Discerning the Spirits: A Guide to Thinking about Christian Worship Today*, in Calvin Institute of Christian Worship Liturgical Studies Series, ed. John D. Witvliet (Grand Rapids MI: Eerdmans, 2003) 128.

17. Marva J. Dawn, *A Royal "Waste" of Time: The Splendor of Worshiping God and Being Church for the World* (Grand Rapids MI: Eerdmans, 1999).

18. Robert E. Webber, *Worship Is a Verb: Celebrating God's Mighty Deeds of Salvation* (Peabody MA: Hendrickson, 2004) 7–8.

19. Ellis, *Approaching God*, 154.

20. N. T. Wright, *Simply Christian: Why Christianity Makes Sense* (New York: HarperCollins, 2006) 148.

21. Witherington, *We Have Seen His Glory*, 36.

22. Dawn, *A Royal "Waste" of Time*, 75, 99, citing Bill McKibben ("Returning God to the Center: Consumerism and the Environmental Threat, in Rodney Clapp, ed., *The Consuming Passion: Christianity and the Consumer Culture* [Downers Grove IL: InterVarsity Press, 1996] 47).

23. Day, *Seeking the Face of God*, 143, 144.

24. Ellis, *Approaching God*, 31.

25. The New Testament in Modern English, trans. J. B. Phillips (New York: Macmillan, 1958).

26. Michael Horton, *A Better Way: Rediscovering the Drama of God-Centered Worship* (Grand Rapids MI: Baker, 2003) 52.

27. Ellis, *Approaching God*, 31.

28. Ibid.

29. Marva J. Dawn, *Reaching Out without Dumbing Down: A Theology of Worship for This Urgent Time* (Grand Rapids MI: Eerdmans, 1995) 4.

30. See, for example, Emil Brunner, *Truth as Encounter*, trans. Amandus W. Loos, David Cairns, T. H. L. Parker, enl. ed. of *The Divine-Human Encounter* (Philadelphia: Westminster Press, 1964).

31. Webber, *Worship Is a Verb*, 26.

32. Ibid., 26–27.

33. N. T. Wright, *Surprised by Hope: Rethinking Heaven, the Resurrection, and the Mission of the Church* (New York: HarperOne, 2008) 208.

34. Douglas John Hall, *Confessing the Faith: Christian Theology in a North American Context* (Minneapolis: Fortress Press, 1996) 123–26.

35. Walter Brueggemann, "Always in the Shadow of Empire," in *Texts that Linger, Words that Explode: Listening to Prophetic Voices*, ed. Patrick D. Miller (Minneapolis: Fortress Press, 2000) 73.

36. Ibid., 87.

37. Stuart Murray, *Church After Christendom*, After Christendom Series (Milton Keynes: Paternoster, 2004) 199.

38. Dawn, *A Royal "Waste" of Time*, 339.

39. Christopher J. Ellis, *Gathering: A Theology and Spirituality of Worship in Free Church Tradition* (London: SCM Press, 2004) 239.

40. John Jefferson Davis, *Worship and the Reality of God: An Evangelical Theology of Real Presence* (Downers Grove IL: InterVarsity Press, 2010) 25.

41. Ibid., 41ff.

42. Ibid., 43, 47.

43. Dawn, *Reaching Out without Dumbing Down*, 72.

44. Ibid., 323.

45. J. Daniel Day, *Seeking the Face of God: Evangelical Worship Reconceived* (Macon GA: Nurturing Faith, 2013) 18.

Chapter 2

What Is Secularization and How Has Evangelical Worship Been Secularized?

In some evangelical circles, "secularism" has become a sort of theological swear word. It is used to refer to anything we don't like and anything with which we disagree. This imprecise usage is unhelpful and does not contribute to clear thinking. For instance, there are some aspects of secularization that most North American evangelicals support, such as the separation of church and state, with a religiously neutral state not favouring one denomination or faith over any other. Once again, as followers of *the* Word we need to be quite precise about what particular words mean.

Defining Secularization

In the most basic sense, secularization simply means the exclusion of religious belief. The secular person, institution, or society does not take into account, or at least not into serious account, spiritual or supernatural matters. Bryan R. Wilson, a prominent Oxford sociologist of religion,[1] described the phenomenon in this way: "religion which once held a general presidency over the concerns of men [sic], and endowed their activities with a sense of sacredness, has increasingly lost this preeminence and influence."[2] Secularization meant "the disappearance of the religious interpretation of the purpose of life . . . . men [sic] have largely ceased to think of—or respond to—the world with a sense of mystery and awe."[3]

Secularization—Individual, Institutional, Societal

Understanding what being secular means is perhaps easier if it is considered in terms of individuals, institutions, and societies.

For the secular *individual*, religion does not, to use Canadian sociologist Reginald Bibby's phrase, constitute "an overarching system of meaning that . . . informs all of life."[4] Faith does not provide the overall interpretation of life, its meaning or purpose. Consequently, at the individual level, to be secular means living *as if* God did not exist or at least with the view that God is not especially relevant to daily life. "The effect of secularization," as David Wells of Gordon-Conwell Theological Seminary puts it, is "to marginalize God, to make what is absolute and transcendent irrelevant to the stuff of everyday life."[5] Whereas Christianity insists that "human beings flourish and are truly happy when they center their lives on God, the source of everything that is true, good and beautiful,"[6] a secular approach to life has a very "different account of human flourishing"[7] that now tends to be understood in terms of the individual's experience of satisfaction,[8] an understanding from which God is noticeably absent.

This approach to life must not be confused with atheism. Theoretical atheism—a reasoned, philosophical conclusion that God does not exist—is relatively uncommon. Usually secular people believe that God (or a "higher power") exists. Most Canadians, Americans, and, for that matter, most Western Europeans affirm this. Often they will also affirm a variety of other more or less recognizably Christian beliefs. The key is that these affirmations have little impact on daily life. This might accurately be described as "practical" atheism—the existence of God is affirmed in theory but denied in practice.

This is quite at odds with the biblical witness, which sees God as the central player in all of life and presents an all-encompassing worldview that interprets the whole of life. In the biblical worldview, my life can only be rightly ordered and whole if I am in right relationship with the God revealed most clearly in Christ, a relationship in which, out of trust, I promise my absolute obedience to Jesus Christ in every part of life. The earliest Christian confession of faith, "Jesus is Lord," meant precisely that Jesus was in charge of every part of life. "Christianity," as Bibby notes, "calls followers to live out the faith in every facet of their lives."[9] For the secular person, that idea is utterly foreign.

At the *institutional* level, secularization means a decline in obviously religious beliefs and practices. Different institutions see this happen in different ways. For churches this can be seen in declining membership and in numbers of those attending Sunday worship. For a college or school that was once explicitly Christian in ethos, evidence of secularization might include the elimination of requirements that faculty members affirm specific doctrinal formulas, the end of mandatory chapel attendance, or the removal of religious images from hallways.

At the *societal* level, secularization means that religion is marginalized, relegated to the "private" sphere of life, with a limited (or no) role in the public sphere. Structures of society that once supported or even privileged religious belief and practice no longer do so.[10] At this level secularization "is the outlook and the values that arise in a society that is no longer taking its bearings from a transcendent order."[11]

Secularization—How Big Is the Problem?

By almost every quantifiable measurement available—from charting declining church and Sunday school attendance to polling on specific beliefs, the number of church closures, levels of public trust in the clergy, a steep decline in the church's participation in mass communication (now dominated by secular rather than faith matters) to falling numbers of baptisms or marriages performed in churches, Western society has become deeply and widely secularized. The reasons are complex and highly debated, as is the question of when precisely the process began and how the phenomenon of secularism is expressed differently in different countries. *That* Western society has become largely secular at the individual, institutional, and societal levels is however not open to serious question. As Walter Brueggemann puts it,

> the church is now faced with a radically *secularized* society, in which the old assumptions of Christendom no longer prevail or command widespread and almost automatic acceptance . . . . the church is no longer a dominant intellectual force in society and no longer can count on cultural reinforcement. The practical signs of that situation include the worry about numbers and dollars in the church, the loss of force in the office of the pastor, and the awareness that our foundational claims of faith are increasingly in deep tension with the dominant visions of the day.[12]

If the measurement tools at our disposal are accurate, the secular approach to life is now the single most significant challenge to Christianity in Western society. That this is indeed the case is a view widely shared across denominational lines, by many of the most profound Christian thinkers of our time—evangelical and otherwise. Canadian United Church theologian Douglas John Hall has made this point repeatedly in many of his books, notably his three-volume theology subtitled *Christian Theology in a North American Context*,[13] and *The End of Christendom and the Future of Christianity*.[14] Charles Taylor is a Canadian philosopher, Templeton Prize winner, and practicing Roman Catholic. His *magnum opus*, *A Secular Age*,[15] examines in depth the change in Western society from a point at which it was virtually impossible not to believe in God to a situation, today, when belief in God is but one option of many. Both John Paul II and Benedict XVI wrote voluminously about the serious challenge posed by secularization, particularly in Western Europe. American United Church of Christ minister and Old Testament scholar Walter Brueggemann has in his dozens of books and hundreds of essays often compared the situation of ancient Israel in exile, surrounded by those who did not know or accept Israel's ancient faith, to the church in contemporary Western society. While the church has obviously not experienced military invasion and deportation, it has gone from a situation where it dominated the culture to being surrounded and vastly outnumbered by those secular folk who neither know nor accept its faith. Brueggemann argues that "the real . . . issue [is] between baptized Christians and those for whom Yahweh has dropped out of the narrative of the world."[16] Edward H. Hammett of the Cooperative Baptist Fellowship in North Carolina is blunt: "we have failed miserably at penetrating the secular world for Christ."[17] American theologian Roger Olson, a Baptist who teaches at Truett Seminary of Baylor University, readily acknowledges,

> I think secularity, a product of modernity, has brought about some good things. I don't believe in shunning everything secular. For example, methodological naturalism in scientific research is secular. There is a sense in which separation of church and state is secular. I happen to think it's also biblical and practical in that it is good for both church and state. It's good theology and good policy. So, "secular" is not always automatically bad.[18]

But secularity, in the sense of "belief that human life can be lived successfully without God or religion," is another thing entirely, and Olson regards this kind of secularity as "an ingredient, if not the main feature, of the modern, Western culture most of us live in on a day-to-day basis."[19] David F. Wells, a Congregationalist minister who is Professor of Historical and Systematic Theology at Gordon-Conwell Theological Seminary just outside Boston, has engaged in a sustained, multi-book analysis and critique of secularization as the most serious challenge the evangelical church faces today.[20]

Differences between Secularization in Europe and Canada/United States

Although the end result at personal, institutional, and societal levels may be similar, it is widely recognized that the historical process of secularization was quite different in the old world and the new. Moreover, the ways in which secularization is expressed or appears are also quite different in Western Europe and North America.

Dr. Martin Marty observes that "the secular has been approached and appropriated in vastly differing ways."[21] He argues persuasively that in continental Western Europe—most notably in France and Germany—the "very first attempts to express (utter) secularity . . . involved a formal and unrelenting attack on gods and churches and a studied striving to replace them."[22] In Britain, by contrast, there was no such sustained campaign, as France saw with Voltaire and during some phases of the French revolution, or in Germany, with figures such as Feuerbach, Marx, and Nietzsche. Instead, faith "and churches were increasingly ignored [with] . . . fewer systematic attempts to replace them."[23] While "In the French Enlightenment of the eighteenth century the frontal attack included the cry, 'Crush the infamous thing' . . . England knew [only] a few minor god-killers . . . people . . . began to ignore Christian claims . . . [and] found that God, Church and Christian teaching were superfluous in their thought and action . . . . The British experience [was] of drift and doubt."[24] Marty argues, however, that the process of secularization in the United States took a much different form from either the continental Western European or British experience. (The Canadian experience of secularity, as in many other aspects of Canadian life, sits somewhere between Europe and the United States. However, Canadian evangelicals, as a much smaller percentage of the population than in the United States, have often tended to look south for models and resources ranging from publishing houses to television ministry broadcasts. Consequently, it can be argued that they have a more American-style experience of secularization than most Canadians, and the larger Anglican [Episcopal], United, and Roman Catholic churches.[25]) While a majority in the United States adhered to the Christianity that came with them from Europe, they transformed this faith and its meaning in what Marty calls "controlled (ambiguous) secularization."[26] In the United States (and I would argue also in Canada), Marty concludes, the "symbols" often remained the same "but their substance or that to which they purportedly referred was often altered."[27] Although "the words [used] remained virtually the same . . . their [meaning] . . . differed."[28] While the words and symbols used remained the same, their content changed and they were given new meanings that supported and endorsed the dominant secular ethos.[29]

The distinguished Oxford sociologist Bryan R. Wilson came to conclusions very similar to Marty's, except that Wilson saw the process of secularization in Britain as more or less the same as in continental Western Europe. In *Religion in Secular Society: A Sociological Comment*, Wilson observed,

> The contrast with which we are presented then is that of a process of secularization in two different societies—America and Europe—which has taken radically divergent forms. That it has been, in each case, a process of secularization, can hardly be in doubt. . . . We are faced then with a traditional society [Europe] in which religious adherence and church attendance have sharply declined during the past eighty years, and a new society [the United States] in which a sharp increase of membership and attendance has taken place over exactly the same period.[30]

His explanation of the difference is virtually identical to Marty's. Whereas in Protestant Europe in general and England in particular, secularization took the form of people simply no longer attending church, in the United States "secularization occurred in quite different ways."[31] In the United States (and by extension, Canada) "Churches have in effect . . . subordinated their distinctively religious values to the values of American [or Canadian] society. Thus, though religious practice . . . increased, the vacuousness of popular religious ideas has also increased, *the content and meaning of religious commitment has been acculturated.*"[32] In the American (and Canadian) experience "secularization drained the religious content, without too radically affecting the form, of religious institutions."[33] The Church does "not dictate social values, but rather reflects those values."[34]

Ross Douthat is a columnist for the *New York Times* and a former senior editor of *The Atlantic*. In his recent book, *Bad Religion: How We Became a Nation of Heretics*, he echoes the more scholarly conclusions of Marty and Wilson pertaining to the United States. A keen observer of contemporary American society and frequent blogger, Douthat concludes that "traditional Christian [teaching] . . . has been transformed"[35] and has become in many respects heretical. He identifies three elements or strands of this heresy—all three of which amount to historic Christian faith being co-opted by secular culture and values. All three strands are prominent within American evangelicalism. One strand is the health and wealth gospel—the "teaching that God wants everyone to get rich."[36] Douthat notes that "the prosperity gospel influences a . . . [large] swatch of American Christianity. It thrives in the Sun Belt and in megachurches."[37] But even the more nuanced forms of it leave little room "for a sustained Christian critique of capitalism's excesses."[38] In particular, Douthat names as examples of this approach Kenneth and Gloria Copeland, Creflo Augustus Dollar Jr., Benny Hinn, Frederick K. C. Price, T. D. Jakes, Larry Burkett, and Joel Osteen,[39] all of whom have significant followings among *both* Canadian and American evangelicals. The second strand Douthat identifies is what he calls the "therapeutic gospel." Commenting on contemporary American society, he argues,

> the Christian teaching that every human soul is unique and precious has been stressed, by the prophets of self-fulfillment and gurus of self-love, at the expense of the equally important teaching that every human soul is fatally corrupted. . . . Absent the latter emphasis, religion becomes a license for egotism and selfishness. . . . The result is a society where pride becomes "healthy self-esteem," vanity becomes "self-improvement," adultery becomes "following your heart," greed and gluttony become "living the American dream."[40]

He notes that in a recent survey of American teenagers, one of the primary characteristics of their "de facto" creed included the belief that "The central goal of life is to be happy and feel good about oneself."[41] The biblical worldview, by contrast, insists that the basis for self-esteem is recognition that we are created and loved by God, and, though fallen, we have been saved by grace. But instead of challenging an approach to life that is clearly contrary to the biblical worldview, much American (and by extension Canadian) Christianity actively *promotes* a therapeutic theology that intertwines the "goals of happiness and self-esteem."[42] The third heretical strand that Douthat notes—also prominent in evangelical circles (more so in the United States than Canada)—is the tendency to identify and confuse nation and faith. Thus,

> many Americans [have been tempted] to regard the United States . . . as a New Israel, a holy nation, a people set apart. This inclination has been woven into every chapter of our nation's history from the Puritan "errand in the wilderness" down to the presidential campaign of Barack

Obama. The language of our politics casts the American story in explicitly religious terms. We're a "promised land" . . . with a "manifest destiny" defined by "American exceptionalism."[43]

Each of the three strands Douthat identifies points to the adoption of a worldview clearly at variance with biblical Christianity—even though that worldview may be couched in traditional biblical and Christian language.

Secularization of Evangelical Common Worship

If the process of secularization in Canada and the United States has often taken the form of transforming churches, "baptizing" a worldview that is foreign to Scripture, a worldview in which, despite the use of traditional language, God and the priorities of God's Kingdom are not central, it should hardly be a surprise that much of the common worship in evangelical churches has also been co-opted.

This is precisely the point made by David F. Wells, a distinguished evangelical scholar at Gordon-Conwell Theological Seminary. He argues that evangelical churches have indeed been significantly co-opted by secularization and that this is evident in, among other things, "the vacuous worship that is so prevalent . . . in the shift from God to the self as the central focus of faith."[44] Wells is by no means alone in raising the alarm about the secularization of much of what happens on Sunday mornings in evangelical churches. His Presbyterian colleague at Gordon-Conwell, John Jefferson Davis, believes "contemporary evangelical Christians have lost their awareness of the *presence of the living and holy God* as the central reality of all true worship."[45] He argues that "the fundamental issue is the recovery of the centrality and reality of God in the worship and life of the evangelical church generally."[46] Robert Webber, who authored more than forty books on worship, particularly among evangelicals, wrote, "I'm discovering many other evangelical Christians today who are also becoming increasingly concerned with a form of worship that centers around man [*sic*] and his needs rather than on God and his work."[47] Marva Dawn, who teaches at Regent College, an interdenominational evangelical school in Vancouver, British Columbia, opines, "when people attend worship for 'what I will get out of it' . . . God is not the center of [such] worship; we are. . . . The result of true worship will be that God will change us, transform us, fashion our character after God's holiness—but only if we worship God and not ourselves."[48] "One of the more disturbing trends in modern worship," writes Ben Witherington III, a Methodist clergyman who teaches at Asbury Theological Seminary, an evangelical school strongly rooted in the tradition of Wesley, "is its *anthropocentric* character and focus. Worship is supposed to be the time when we take our eyes off ourselves . . . and focus on God."[49] He concludes, "What is blurred all too often in modern worship is the radical distinction between God and humankind."[50] The preeminent biblical scholar Walter Brueggemann observes that Jesus was driven out of the synagogue in Nazareth, a "worship that echo[ed] the dominant culture,"[51] and comments, "The practice of faithful worship is more odd than we often take it to be, familiar as it is to us. In recent time much of that oddness has been relinquished in the church, in a seductive attempt to be current, popular, alternative, or entertaining."[52]

Secularization is not only the single biggest challenge facing Christianity in contemporary Western society but has also deeply compromised much of evangelicalism in general—and evangelical worship in particular—in both Canada and the United States. This, in and of itself, should be a matter of grave concern. But given the influence of American evangelicalism in particular on evangelicalism worldwide, it is doubly a cause for anxiety.

How Evangelical Common Worship Has Been Secularized

Worship is secularized whenever the focus of that worship is no longer God, specifically the God whom we know best in Jesus Christ. This happens even if traditional words, actions, symbols, or music are retained. Or, to draw from the understanding of the purpose of worship in chapter 1, worship is secularized whenever it "*serve[s] any other purpose except the glory of God.*"[53] Whenever the end of worship is something—anything—other than worship,[54] worship has become secularized.

What then are some of the indicators that show common worship that has been co-opted and is no longer focused exclusively on God, worship in which the words and symbols have been retained but filled with new, secularized meaning? Following are five such indicators, warning signals, that are seen frequently in evangelical common worship.

First, when worship is driven by pragmatic concerns, it almost always signifies some degree of secularization. Often this pragmatism is indicated by the use of phrases such as "well, it works" or "you can't argue with success" or "it brings in the young people." In each case, these phrases usually refer to the numbers of people attending Sunday worship. But common worship is *not* about the numbers. The wider society, which does not have God at its centre, measures success by the numbers. But emphatically this is *not* how God measures success. If the people of God start measuring success by the numbers, they have, to that degree, adopted a worldview that is not centred on God.[55] *God's measurement of success has always been faithfulness, obedience to his will.*[56] By the secular—apart from God—way of measuring success, many of the chief characters in the biblical accounts failed. For example, the preaching of the great prophets of ancient Israel was widely ignored or ridiculed. By secular measurement, even Jesus was a notable failure at the time of his death. After three years of public ministry, he had merely 120 followers in Jerusalem (Acts 2:15)—not exactly a megachurch!

When we start measuring success by the numbers, we are on spiritually thin ice. The question from a biblical, God-centred perspective is not "How many people were in church this morning?" but "What did they get when they got there?" or "Did they actually worship God?" Have we evangelicals forgotten that Jesus taught "the gate is wide and the road is easy that leads to destruction, and there are many who take it . . . the gate is narrow and the road is hard that leads to life, and there are few who find it" (Matt 7:13-14)? Why on earth do we insist then that big attendance figures somehow indicate we are on the right track and our Sunday worship is just as it should be? Perhaps it's the reverse. "Sound doctrine" is not popular, as the Second Letter to Timothy indicates; people prefer to "accumulate for themselves teachers to suit their own desires" (2 Tim 4:3). Should we be surprised that it is possible to draw large crowds to hear their self-centred, environmentally unsustainable, wasteful, self-absorbed, socially unconcerned lifestyles endorsed, justified, and declared righteous? In light of Paul's warning to Timothy, are such numbers, such "popularity," not to be regarded as deeply disturbing? The purpose of worship "is not to gain numbers nor for our churches to be successful. Rather the entire reason for our worship of God is that God deserves it."[57] J. Daniel Day makes what to some evangelicals will seem shocking but is in reality a deeply biblical suggestion about faithful pastoring:

> I . . . have found a counter-cultural joy in leading people to do what we believed to be right even if it did not produce numerical growth . . . . one of the most valorous acts a pastor can do in many churches is to lead the church to engage in worship that is really about God. . . . The number of those in attendance is ultimately beyond our control. Our proper task

is much more humble. . . . Ours is to offer worship that really is about God.⁵⁸

Closely related to the first indicator of secularized worship is the second: a "consumer-driven" approach to common worship. Evangelicals are well aware that in a capitalist society people have choices and will patronize shops and services where what they want and prefer is readily available at the cheapest price. Unfortunately, this awareness has often been transmuted into the church's worship. Congregations invest time, energy, and money into providing worship services that give the consumer whatever she or he wants (affirmation, self-fulfillment, finding oneself, and useful advice on relationships, finances, or raising children). This is to be offered at little or no cost. There is no expectation that the recipient will contribute of his or her time to the life and work of the church, let alone—and much more important—is there much suggestion that the sovereign God lays claim to one's entire life. This is the "cheap grace" that Dietrich Bonhoeffer decried: "the preaching of forgiveness without requiring repentance, baptism without church discipline, Communion without confession."⁵⁹ This consumer-driven approach secularizes worship by moving the focus from God to the wants and demands of the worshipper. Christopher J. Ellis, former Principal of Bristol Baptist College in England comments that while "Worship . . . is *supposed* to be about what God wants . . . often it is about what the worshippers want . . . . consumers gather, ready yet again to assert their requirements and express their choices."⁶⁰ Ben Witherington III points out,

> The consumer approach to worship puts the emphasis almost entirely on the wrong syllable. It leads to pastors desperately seeking to change . . . worship . . . in an attempt to attract a bigger crowd, the theory being that worship should be a matter of giving the people what they want. . . . This is completely wrong. Worship is a matter of giving to God what he desires and requires of us.⁶¹

Witherington relates a story from his home church that makes the distinction between the consumer-driven approach to worship and the genuine article:

> There was an elderly woman in my home church who could barely see or hear. Yet there she was each Sunday . . . participating in worship with vigor. At one point, a young woman asked her why she was there, since

she couldn't really hear much of what was being said or see much of what was happening. Her reply was memorable: "I'm not here for what I can get out of the service but for what I can give. I get the bulletin mailed to me and I get out my magnifying glass and read it through, and then I read the Scriptures and the hymns we will sing. I think and pray through what may be God's Word for me in this. So when I come to the service, I'm ready to worship, and I give that to God, even though I'm getting back perhaps less than some . . . ." The young woman was stunned. Caught up in the consumer mentality of many, and applying it to worship, she had just assumed that one chose a worship service . . . based on what one could get out of it, not on where God might be best pleased to receive our worship and service.[62]

Marva Dawn echoes both Ellis and Witherington, arguing, "What . . . people want might not be good for them, and . . . churches are in the business of forming Christians, not catering to consumerist choices."[63] Similarly, Thomas Long, a gifted preacher and professor of homiletics at Chandler School of Theology at Emory University, warns,

> while authentic worship will meet people's needs and thus will be attractive to people, not everything that attracts people to the sanctuary is authentic worship. Indeed, it is easier . . . to create events that we *call* "worship," events that attract curious crowds of people, who are drawn not genuinely to worship God but to be entertained, flattered, given cost-free therapy, provided with short-term practical advice for living, or offered any of the countless other superficial incentives that will gather people for a while. So if we base decisions about congregational worship on what-do-people-say-they-want-in-worship "market research," matching worship styles to current fashion, taste and popular preference, we will distort worship beyond recognition and mangle it into something alien: simply a mirror of the culture's current fancy.[64]

A third feature of secularized worship is a focus, especially in preaching, on meeting "felt needs." Obviously every preacher wants to demonstrate the relevance of Scripture to daily life. As evangelicals we do, after all, see Scripture as *the* authoritative guide to life. The problem arises when sermons become focused more on the problems than on God's word to his people, when the direction of preaching is more from our problems to Scripture than the other way around. It's a subtle shift, but one that tends to change the emphasis from God and God's word to us, to thinking of God and God's Word as tools—albeit wonderful tools, but still tools—for helping us deal with life. For example, a sermon about how Scripture gives useful tips and principles for improving one's finances puts the emphasis in an entirely different place than a sermon that proclaims that God is the owner of all things by right of creation and challenges listeners to look at how this reality is reflected in their finances. How do I spend my money? How much do I give to the church's work, to feed the poor, or to care for the sick and oppressed? Do I own stocks in companies whose labour or environmental practices are unethical and contrary to Kingdom values? How do I teach my children about money as a follower of Jesus? What do I need to do to ensure that my financial affairs are in line with God's will? Michael Horton puts it this way:

> Our contemporaries are searching frantically for a narrative large enough to give some purpose to their lives, so that (ironically) the more we cater to their immediate cravings, the less we actually contribute to what they're hoping to find: some enduring sense of who they are and where they fit into something larger than themselves.[65]

A fourth indicator of secularized worship in contemporary evangelicalism can often—ironically—be confusing common worship with evangelism. Evangelism is, as we have already seen, a "by-product" of common worship. It is not common worship itself. Even something as incredibly important, something having such eternal significance as evangelism must not be confused with common worship, the *sole* focus of which is God and the *sole* purpose of which is the acknowledgment of God's supreme worth. When worship and evangelism become confused, the focus begins slowly to move from God to the potential converts in the congregation.

For much of the church's long history, the notion that common worship was about evangelism would have been nearly incomprehensible to most Christians. The glimpses we are given of the church's worship both in the New Testament and the sub-apostolic era involve the people of God, not outsiders. In the patristic era, even those who were already professing Christians but had not yet been baptized were permitted to attend *only* the service of the word but were dismissed before the celebration of the Lord's Supper—never mind those who were not Christian at all! Evidently there was in the early church a strong sense that *only* believers could genuinely and truly worship God.

The move to make evangelism the focus of worship is a recent phenomenon in the church's history. It stemmed in large degree from the pragmatism of the American frontier experience. In the context of remote, scattered homesteads, it was often impossible to establish regular common worship and congregational life. Infrequent but large camp meeting gatherings became normative. Not surprisingly given that many in the frontier were very far indeed from Christian faith or practice, these meetings had a strong focus on evangelism. The problem was that this confused common worship with evangelism, indeed saw worship as primarily a prelude to and in service of the altar call.

Charles Finney, a nineteenth-century American evangelist, ministered not in the remote frontier but in the urban centres of New England as well as New York City. He insisted on "new measures," the key test of which was whether they "worked" in bringing people to faith. Finney—who had limited theological education—apparently did not recognize the inherent danger in making theology and theological truth subservient to evangelistic outcomes. Certainly it cannot be denied that many apparently came to genuine and life-changing faith in Christ during Finney's meetings. The Holy Spirit can, thankfully, do his work despite our theological errors! But it is never safe or wise to substitute pragmatism for the truth, and there were long-term consequences to Finney's confusion of worship and evangelism. It is not difficult to trace a line from the frontier camp meetings and Finney's widely imitated approach to the worship services of many contemporary evangelical churches, which continue to see "whatever works evangelistically" as the self-evidently correct approach to worship. "What works" is, however, most emphatically *not* a theological or biblical category! A focus on "what works" inevitably means an increasingly anthropocentric focus in common worship, since what "works" and draws crowds of potential converts is worship that is concerned with how the worshipper feels.[66]

Confusing common worship and evangelism presents other theological difficulties too. It seems to ignore the reality that genuine worship must be worship in "spirit and in truth" (John 4:24)—in the end only those who confess him as Lord can truly worship God. J. Daniel Day notes, "the New Testament does not authorize the conversion of church worship gatherings into evangelistic meetings. To the contrary, the repeated impression from every biblical glimpse into the gatherings of the earliest Christians is that these were meetings of and for the faithful, not the outsider."[67] Roger Prentice, long-time chaplain to Acadia University, writes, "the worship service is a gathering of the faithful. It is not a time for 'evangelism,' as important as that may be, but rather it is the sole time for the Christian to gather with other Christians to offer their corporate worship to God as the Church."[68] Moreover, when evangelism is thought of as something that happens during Sunday morning worship, the responsibility of every individual believer to bear witness to Christ by words and actions in daily life tends to be quickly forgotten. Evangelism becomes something for which the minister is responsible on Sunday mornings. This attitude stands in opposition to Christ's injunction in the Great Commission. It also stands contrary to the practice of the early church, for there is little evidence the early church saw common worship as the venue for evangelistic activities. Instead, evangelism largely happened as individual believers told friends and family what they had experienced, through public proclamation and debate in the open marketplace of ideas,[69] and when miraculous events were explained to astonished bystanders.

Another theological difficulty that arises from the confusion of common worship and evangelism is the lack of any opportunity for response—other than responding to the "altar call." Even the offering becomes something to "get out of the way" so as not to blunt the altar call's being the sharp, high point of the service. But this simply does not align with the models for worship with which we are presented in Scripture. There, inevitably, the gathering of God's people in worship led to response by God's people—from giving of financial resources to meet the needs of the poor, to going out to live out the teaching that had been given. *God's people* do not respond to common worship by *becoming God's people*. They already are. Now they need to *act* on that reality.

Finally, confusing worship with evangelism tends to reduce the amount and depth of serious teaching from Scripture since all attention is directed to inviting people to faith in Christ. Is it any wonder that so many evangelicals have but a rudimentary knowledge of Scripture when week in and week out, year in and year out, they hear sermons that have only this one subject? How do we expect people to live out their faith in a complex, secular society—which often has a multitude of criticisms and misconceptions about our faith—without giving them anything more than altar-call sermons every Sunday to equip them? In many evangelical churches, one could go for years without hearing a single sermon that thoughtfully addresses some of the criticisms raised against Christian faith in our society, or that exegetes difficult texts in Scripture (particularly those in which violence plays a prominent role). In some evangelical churches, one could easily get the impression that the Bible has nothing to say about unjust economic systems, unfair trade treaties, political corruption, or the environment. When was the last time you remember hearing a sermon in an evangelical pulpit that explained the Trinity and tried to show its relevance to daily life? Or a sermon that outlined the biblical concept of vocation and work? J. Daniel Day comments on how the switch from understanding worship as worship to seeing worship as evangelism resulted in deleterious changes for evangelical churches and clergy:

> [Ministers] whose strength was as teacher or resident scholar or gentle shepherd were now less favored than preachers who . . . stir listeners' emotions and effectively exhort sinners to "come to Jesus" . . . . Exposure to the entire canon of scripture and the wide range of Christian doctrine was thereby diminished in deference to the new evangelistic mandate.[70]

Let us, for the sake of argument, set aside all theological considerations for a moment. On a strictly practical level, in a secular society, the notion that Sunday worship is the time to issue evangelistic appeals is ridiculous. Secular people are rarely to be found attending morning worship. The model of evangelism happening *within* the church building, *during* worship services only developed when Christendom held sway, when there was great social, family, or political pressure to attend church services and little "competition" for people's attention on Sundays—think Sunday "blue laws" that required businesses to be closed and frequently kept cinemas, theatres, recreation, and sports facilities shuttered.[71] But Christendom is gone, and this "get-them-into-the-church" model for evangelism—which was theologically dubious to begin with—is gone with it. It almost always means issuing altar calls to the already converted. What is the point of that? If we are truly committed to evangelism, we need to return to the incarnational model[72] of the early church. This is common worship that sends the people of God back out into the wider world to bear witness to the risen Christ, rather than expecting those outside the faith to cross a multitude of cultural and social boundaries to come to us in a place where we are comfortable.

A final indicator of secularized worship is a focus on "experience," that is to say, the affective or emotional consciousness or awareness of God's presence. Certainly such experiences can and often do happen during common worship, and should be received thankfully as a gift from God to his people. The problem comes when such experiences became the *raison d'être* for worship, the goal of worship, or the yardstick by which worship is measured as having been "real" or not. When *any* of these things happen, the focus of worship has shifted from God to a by-product of genuine worship, in this case the affective experience of God, and to that degree it is secularized. A focus on experience creates a cascade of other problems as well. When "experience" becomes the focus, there is a tendency to devalue loving, honouring, and worshipping God with the mind. "Heart" is valued over "head" instead of seeing that God desires both to be subject to him. Those leading worship may very well find themselves feeling pressure—overt or covert—to ensure that the congregation has an emotional experience of God every Sunday. In worst-case scenarios, this can lead to constant innovation and showmanship in a desperate effort to evoke an emotional response each week.

Why Does It Matter?

Some readers may at this point be asking, "But does all this really matter? In the end, what difference does it make?" It matters because there is so much at stake.

First and foremost, evangelicals need to return the focus of common worship to God because it is the right thing to do. It is truth. Evangelicals take truth seriously. And we take Scripture as our authority in matters of faith and practice—Scripture is our source of truth in these matters. And Scripture makes it clear that the core human problem is our insistence on doing things our way—which we regard as "freedom"—instead of submitting ourselves to God and his way. Paradoxically, slavery to God means real freedom. If we accept this as truth, then we have no choice but that our worship should reflect this truth, worship that unquestionably acknowledges God's sovereignty and lordship over our lives. The secularization of much evangelical worship matters because it denies this truth. Genuine worship is about pleasing and adoring God—period, full stop. It is most emphatically not about the worshipper; it is about the one who is worshipped.

Second, common worship that has been secularized matters because it will not do well in shaping worshippers and their worldview according to Scripture. "As much as we might wish it were otherwise," writes Nathan Nettleton, "most of the people in our congregations do not spend a lot of time studying the Bible, discussing Christian theology and practice or attending Christian education programmes. For better or worse, most of them learn most of what they know about the Christian faith within the worship service."⁷³ Given this reality, we urgently need common worship that is founded on a carefully thought out theology of worship—rather than flying by the seat of our pants.

Third, common worship matters because the very survival of the church—as something distinct from the wider culture—depends on it. As a nation, ancient Israel was dwarfed and surrounded by larger nations that did not worship Yahweh. There was a constant temptation toward assimilation. That pressure became even more acute during the exile, when large numbers of Jews found themselves forced to live far away from their homeland, a tiny minority among those who neither knew nor cared much about their faith. The only way to avoid assimilation was to insist on the maintenance of worship that remained clearly and consciously distinct from the wider society. (That is one reason behind the ferocious insistence on the importance of Sabbath observance.) Being co-opted would spell disaster. As a minority in a secular culture, Christians in the Western world also court disaster if our worship is co-opted, not by the worship of the Baals of the Palestinians or the gods of Babylonia, but by our surrounding culture.

Finally, secularized worship seriously hinders our ability to reach others with the gospel. It fails to equip our people for doing the work of evangelism outside the church walls. Partly this is because such compromised worship fails to shape us biblically, so we are left with little to say to the wider society. Such worship does not challenge either those inside *or* outside the faith with the profound differences between the wider culture and what it means to follow Jesus Christ. Secularized worship grants permission for the focus to remain on "me" rather than God. Secularized worship also hinders the evangelistic mission of the church because it tends to leave evangelism to the clergy, the "professionals," on Sunday mornings.

Being Clear about What Isn't Being Said

Aesthetics and Worship

Please do not conclude that what you are reading is merely a "rant" directed at so-called "contemporary" worship. Let me be clear. What I *am* saying is that theologically informed common worship *must* always be focused on God, not the worshipper, *must* always have certain elements present and present in a certain logical order, and *must* not be co-opted by the surrounding secular culture.

There are many different, legitimate styles or approaches to worship. Given the diversity of human beings, varying gifts that God may give to individuals in every different congregation, and widely different cultures and situations in which the church finds itself, that is hardly unexpected. Indeed, it may be seen as part of the marvelous expression of God's creativity and the creativity he has given us to exercise that God can be and is worshipped in so many different ways. All of us have aesthetic preferences. I know I certainly do. Some churches are aesthetically "Bach," others "country," some "Celtic." I have attended worship services where I was aesthetically horrified—but that was ultimately unimportant because there was a clearly thought out, biblically based theology of worship underlying what was happening. On the other hand, I have also attended worship services that were aesthetically superb but seemed spiritually lifeless. Aesthetics and differing tastes are *not* the issue. It is vital to realize "We're not talking here about mere differences in taste . . . but about judgements of fittingness. We're wrestling with questions of integrity: are we upholding the integrity of the gospel and of Christian worship even as we translate them into fresh cultural idioms?"[74]

Genuine Faith

Let me be clear. I am *not* saying that there isn't genuine faith in evangelical churches that exhibit some or all of the features of secularized worship. There is genuine faith—often profound faith. Nor, mindful of Paul's injunctions in Romans 14, am I suggesting that these issues are, normally, of such a nature as to mean breaking fellowship—as long as the critical confession of Christ's lordship is still present. What I am saying is that we *can do worship much better.* We *can* have evangelical worship that does not sail perilously close to the edge of our becoming chaplains to the secular culture around us, worship that challenges instead of fosters or confirms a secular approach to life, worship that is in every respect carefully and thoughtfully informed by a clearly evangelical theology of worship.

Notes

1. Wilson (1926–2004) was a long-time fellow of All Souls College and author of more than a dozen books. He was president of the International Society for the Sociology of Religion (1971–1975) and editor of the *Journal for the Scientific Study of Religion*. He held honorary doctorates from both Oxford and the Catholic University of Leuven in Belgium.

2. Bryan R. Wilson, *Religion in Secular Society: A Sociological Comment* (London: C. A. Watts, 1966; repr., Middlesex, England: Penguin, 1969) 78.

3. Ibid.

4. Reginald W. Bibby, *Fragmented Gods: The Poverty and Potential of Religion in Canada* (Toronto: Irwin Publishing, 1987) 140.

5. David F. Wells, *No Place for Truth: Or Whatever Happened to Evangelical Theology?* (Grand Rapids MI: Eerdmans, 1993) 7.

6. Miroslav Volf, *A Public Faith: How Followers of Christ Should Serve the Common Good* (Grand Rapids MI: Brazos, 2011) 58.

7. Ibid.

8. Ibid., 59, 60.

9. Bibby, *Fragmented Gods*, 140.

10. The end of a privileged position and relationship with such structures is part of the long, slow death of the Christendom model that prevailed in Western society from the time of Constantine. In the New Testament, the pictures we are given of the church are always of a minority functioning within the wider civil society. For the first three hundred years of its existence, this was the model of the Christian church. It was a small, sometimes persecuted, but often merely ignored group within the wider population. Then, after his supposed conversion, the Emperor Constantine (d. 337) made Christianity a legal religion of the Roman Empire. In 380, the Emperor Theodosius made Christianity the sole legal religion. This "Constantinian settlement" (which perhaps more accurately should be called the "Theodosian settlement") placed the Christian church in a privileged position in which it worked, hand in glove, with the state. This model—Christendom—was a profound deviation from the model of the church in the New Testament where the church is pictured as a gathered community of those who have chosen to confess Jesus as Lord. But under Christendom, with Christianity as the only legal faith, a status supported if need be by lethal government force, being a Christian became more or less automatically equated with being a citizen. Being a Christian often had little to do with any lively faith in Christ, while being a non-Christian was at best to be tolerated. Laws favoured "Christians." In many cases, laws restricted many professions to Christians and denied higher education and political offices to non-Christians. Everyone, Christian or otherwise, paid taxes to support the church. Non-Christians often were restricted as to where they could live, when they could travel, and how they could dress. Even after Christianity in the Western world split into two major groupings—Roman Catholic and Protestant—the Christendom pattern remained. Every country of Western Europe had an official state church, whether Roman Catholic or some variety of Protestant, and woe betide those who did not belong. The end of Christendom is not to be lamented but welcomed as a return to the model of church seen in the New Testament—the church as the followers of Jesus who work, in love, not by force or compulsion, to see the Kingdom realized and to invite, not compel, pressure, or coerce others to join them in following him.

11. ~~Wells, *No Place for Truth*, 80.~~

12. Walter Brueggemann, "Testimony as a Decentered Mode of Preaching," in *Cadences of Home: Preaching among Exiles* (Louisville: Westminster John Knox, 1997) 40–41.

13. Douglas John Hall, *Thinking the Faith: Christian Theology in a North American Context* (Minneapolis: Fortress, 1989); *Professing the Faith: Christian Theology in a North American Context* (Minneapolis: Fortress, 1993); *Confessing the Faith: Christian Theology in a North American Context* (Minneapolis: Fortress, 1996).

14. Douglas John Hall, *The End of Christendom and the Future of Christianity* (Philadelphia: Trinity Press International, 1997).

15. Charles Taylor, *A Secular Age* (Cambridge MA: Belknap Press of Harvard University Press, 2007).

16. Walter R. Brueggemann, "Always in the Shadow of Empire," in *Texts that Linger, Words that Explode: Listening to Prophetic Voices* (Minneapolis: Fortress, 2000) 87. For a valuable exploration of this theme in Brueggemann, see J. Derrick Marshall, "The Ethics of Exile," M.A. thesis, St. Paul's University, Ottawa, 2008.

17. Edward H. Hammett, *The Gathered and Scattered Church: Equipping Believers for the 21st Century* (Macon GA: Smyth & Helwys, 1999) 6.

18. Roger E. Olson, "How Secularized Has American Evangelical Christianity Become," http://www.patheos.com/blogs/rogereolson/2013/01/how-secularized-has-american-evangelical-christianity-become/.

19. Ibid.

20. See for example Wells, *No Place for Truth* (cited above) *God in the Wasteland: The Reality of Truth in a World of Fading Dreams* (Grand Rapids MI: Eerdmans, 1994); *Above All Earthly Pow'rs: Christ in a Postmodern World* (Grand Rapids MI: Eerdmans, 2006).

21. Martin E. Marty, *The Modern Schism: Three Paths to the Secular* (New York: Harper & Row, 1969; repr., Eugene OR: Wipf and Stock, 2012) 10.

22. Ibid., 10.

23. Ibid., 10, 18, 47.

24. Ibid., 18–19.

25. See for example Peter Berger, Grace Davie, and Effie Fokas, *Religious America, Secular Europe? A Theme and Variations* (Farnham, Surrey: Ashgate Publishing, 2008); Mark A. Noll, *What Happened to Christian Canada?* (Vancouver: Regent College Publishing, 2007).

26. Martin E. Marty, *The Modern Schism*, 10.

27. Ibid., 100–101.

28. Ibid.

29. Ibid., 137.

30. Wilson, *Religion in Secular Society*, 118.

31. Ibid., 138.

32. Ibid., 122, emphasis added.

33. Ibid., 252.

34. Ibid., 115.

35. Ross Douthat, *Bad Religion: How We Became a Nation of Heretics* (New York: Free Press, 2012) 5.

36. Ibid.

37. Ibid., 101.

38. Ibid., 199.

39. Ibid., 198.

40. Ibid., 5.

41. Douthat, *Bad Religion*, 232–33, citing Christian Smith and Melinda Lundquist Denton, *Soul Searching: The Religious and Spiritual Lives of American Teenagers* (New York: Oxford University Press, 2005) 162–63.

42. Douthat, *Bad Religion*, 234.

43. Ibid., 249.

44. Wells, *No Place for Truth*, 95.

45. John Jefferson Davis, *Worship and the Reality of God: An Evangelical Theology of Real Presence* (Downers Grove IL: InterVarsity Press, 2010) 100.

46. Ibid., 12.

47. Robert E. Webber, *Worship is a Verb: Celebrating God's Mighty Deeds of Salvation* (Peabody MA: Hendrickson, 2004) 66.

48. Marva J. Dawn, *Reaching Out without Dumbing Down: A Theology of Worship for This Urgent Time* (Grand Rapids MI: Eerdmans, 1995) 124.

49. Ben Witherington III, *We Have Seen His Glory: A Vision of Kingdom Worship*, in Calvin Institute of Christian Worship Liturgical Studies Series, ed. John D. Witvliet (Grand Rapids MI: Eerdmans, 2010) 21.

50. Ibid., 22.

51. Walter Brueggemann, "A Welcome for the Others," in *Mandate to Difference: An Invitation to the Contemporary Church* (Louisville: Westminster John Knox, 2007) 69.

52. Walter Brueggemann, "Spirit Led Imagination," in *Mandate to Difference*, 117.

53. Simon Chan, *Liturgical Theology: The Church as Worshiping Community* (Downers Grove IL: InterVarsity Press, 2006) 53.

54. Ibid.

55. This point is made forcefully by former megachurch pastor Tim Suttle in his superb book *Shrink: Faithful Ministry in a Church-Growth Culture* (Grand Rapids MI: Zondervan, 2014).

56. This understanding of what constitutes true success is a theme that appears repeatedly and in numerous variations throughout Scripture. Abraham is commended not for his vast herds or many servants but because he believes God (Gen 15:6). Samuel, told to anoint a king to replace Saul, is initially impressed by the numbers—in this case the height of David's older brother, Eliab—but is told that number is irrelevant. When David, chosen from obscurity to become Israel's greatest king, is praised by Scripture it is not for any "numbers"—his height (or lack thereof), the number of men in his army, or his wealth—but for being a man after God's own heart (1 Sam 13:14; Acts 13:22). The great prophets of Israel rarely had "success" in terms of the numbers of people who repented and returned to Yahweh, but they are nevertheless set forth as exemplary models. Their "success" consisted of their dogged obedience to God, despite death threats, persecution, and mistreatment. In the parable of the talents (Matt 25:14-30), it is not the size of the increase in the money entrusted to them by their master for which two of the three servants receive praise. Rather it is for being "good and faithful" (25:21, 23, AV). The risen and ascended Jesus promises the Christians in Smyrna that those who are "*faithful* unto death [emphasis added]" will receive "a crown of life" (Rev 2:10, AV). It seems that God even deliberately chooses the

obscure, the weak, and the few to accomplish his ends. Gideon finds himself being told to reduce dramatically the number of troops who will join him in repelling the Midianites. Paul's prayers for relief from an unnamed "thorn in the flesh" receives God's answer that "my grace is sufficient for thee: for my strength is made perfect in weakness" (2 Cor 12:7, 9, AV).

57. Keith G. Jones, "On Abandoning Public Worship," in *Currents in Baptistic Theology of Worship Today*, ed. Keith J. Jones, Parush R. Parushev (Prague: International Baptist Theological Seminary, 2007) 8.

58. J. Daniel Day, *Seeking the Face of God: Evangelical Worship Reconceived* (Macon GA: Nurturing Faith, 2013) 276, 279.

59. Dietrich Bonhoeffer, *The Cost of Discipleship*, rev. ed., trans. R. H. Fuller, Irmgard Booth (New York: MacMillian, 1949; repr., New York: MacMillan, 1963) 47.

60. Christopher J. Ellis, *Gathering: A Theology and Spirituality of Worship in Free Church Tradition* (London: SCM Press, 2004) 2, emphasis added.

61. Witherington, *We Have Seen His Glory*, 16.

62. Ibid.

63. Marva J. Dawn, *A Royal "Waste" of Time: The Splendor of Worshiping God and Being Church for the World* (Grand Rapids MI: Eerdmans, 1999) 195.

64. Thomas G. Long, *Beyond the Worship Wars: Building Vital and Faithful Worship* (Herdon VA: The Alban Institute, 2001) 17.

65. Michael Horton, *A Better Way: Rediscovering the Drama of God-Centered Worship* (Grand Rapids MI: Baker, 2003) 52.

66. Finney's theology had other dubious elements as well. It overemphasized human freedom over divine sovereignty, had a limited view of the extent and depth of sin, and tended strongly to support the "Christendom model" that saw "church" (that is, common worship) as the location where evangelism happened. Instead of the Kingdom of God—the focus of the preaching of Jesus, one aspect of which involved evangelism—being central, evangelism *itself* became the first, most important, and central thrust of Christian life. Social justice took a distant second place. In some cases, social action eventually came to be justifiable among evangelicals only insofar as it was a prelude to evangelism. Finney's ecclesiology was also extremely low, to the point of being almost nonexistent. John Witvliet notes, "Any organic notion of the nature of the church was suppressed in favour of the important personal decision that individuals need to make to bring about their conversion . . . . the individual was emphasized over against the catholic church . . . . the existence of the church [was made] more dependent on an individual's decision for Christ than Christ's ongoing presence in the world" (*Worship Seeking Understanding: Windows into Christian Practice* [Grand Rapids MI: Baker, 2013] 194–95).

67. Day, *Seeking the Face of God*, 35.

68. Roger H. Prentice, *Hymns at Heaven's Gate: The Use & Abuse of Hymns* (Kentville, N.S.: Gaspereau Press, 2008) 163.

69. Peter's speech on the Day of Pentecost (Acts 2) was not delivered in the context of a worship service. Acts 17 has the apostle Paul arguing in the synagogue (presumably NOT during Sabbath worship!) and the marketplace, and debating with both Epicurean and Stoic philosophers. Here also is Paul's speech to Athenians in the areopagus, the most important public space in the city.

70. Day, *Seeking the Face of God*, 36.

71. The first such "blue law," not surprisingly, was enacted by the Emperor Constantine in AD 321. It ordered workshops to be closed "on the day of the Sun." Perhaps the most extreme example of the enforcement of a day of rest was in some of the remote Western Scottish islands, where even swings in parks were tied up on Sunday to prevent children from using them!

72. "Incarnational" in the sense of reflecting the example of God in Christ. God did not stand apart from estranged humanity but came to us and to where we were in the most literal sense of those words, when in Jesus God became a human being.

73. Nathan Nettleton, "Making Meaning in Worship: Ritual and Narrative Structure," in *Currents in Baptistic Theology of Worship Today*, ed. Keith G. Jones, Parush R. Parushev (Prague: Published by International Baptist Theological Seminary, 2007) 87.

74. Cornelius Pantinga, Jr., and Sue Rozeboom, *Discerning the Spirits: A Guide to Thinking about Christian Worship Today*, in Calvin Institute of Christian Worship Liturgical Studies Series, ed. John D. Witvliet (Grand Rapids MI: Eerdmans, 2003) 50.

Chapter 3

Principles for an Evangelical Theology of Worship

Much like the word "worship," the word "evangelical" has become slippery, even among those who use it to describe themselves. Much as with the word "worship," it is often assumed that everyone agrees about the meaning of the term "evangelical." In practice, however, the term "evangelical" is applied loosely and imprecisely to so many different things that it can signify almost anything and everything, which results in its meaning nothing in particular.

Scholars have used oceans of ink in efforts to define precisely the word "evangelical" and to determine its boundaries. Reporters for the mass media, often secular in worldview and rarely having any training or education in matters theological, sometimes seem to use the word "evangelical" to suggest or imply that something or someone is cult-like or intellectually challenged. "Evangelical" often is applied indiscriminately to individuals and groups as widely differing as Jerry Falwell and the "moral majority" to Jim Wallis and Sojourners, from Jimmy Carter to George W. Bush. Perhaps there is no clearer indication of confusion over any word's meaning than when that word starts having ever more adjectives attached to it by those who use it to describe themselves. It is commonplace today to find people describing themselves not simply as "evangelical" but also as catholic, liberal, progressive, open, green, left wing, neo, charismatic, moderate, conservative, or post-conservative evangelical.

Just as with the term "worship," the most important step in trying to think clearly, deeply, and carefully about anything is to know *what* one is thinking about. Before we can begin a discussion of principles for evangelical worship, we have to understand what the word "evangelical" means or, at the very least, how the word is going to be used here.

The Meaning of the Word "Evangelical"

The word "evangelical" comes from the Greek word εὐαγγέλιον, which means "good news." In the New Testament this is specifically the "good news" of the salvation, freedom, and wholeness made possible by the life, death, resurrection, and ascension of Jesus Christ. The four canonical Gospels, being accounts of the life of Jesus, were therefore respectively titled "The Good News According to . . ." Matthew, Mark, Luke and John.

The medieval church in Western Europe used the term "evangelical" in a much different way from Scripture. The church taught that the words of Jesus in Matthew 19:21 constituted three "evangelical counsels" or "counsels of perfection." These attributes or virtues were not binding on all (that is to say they were not needful in order to attain eternal life) but were acts that went beyond the minimum requirements of Scripture. Hence these counsels—chastity, poverty, and obedience—were vowed by those entering religious orders, and those whose lives notably exhibited these characteristics were referred to as evangelical.

With the sixteenth-century Reformation in Europe, a new meaning was attached yet again to the word "evangelical." It came to be used, among German speakers in general and Lutherans in particular (who were following the usage of Martin Luther himself), as more or less synonymous with the word "Protestant." This particular usage is still seen in the names of many Lutheran denominations worldwide. In both Canada and the United States, the largest Lutheran bodies (respectively The Evangelical Lutheran Church in Canada and The Evangelical Lutheran Church in America) use the word "evangelical" in this sense.

A distinctive evangelical "movement," a movement within Protestantism that had recognizable and distinct theological emphases, can be traced to a series of events beginning in the 1730s, occurring more or less simultaneously in both Great Britain and Ireland and within the thirteen American colonies. The story is complex and involved a great deal of cross-fertilization between events and people through published accounts and personal contacts across the Atlantic. American church historian Mark Noll writes, "During the middle third of the eighteenth century, a similar series of interconnected renewal movements arose in England, Wales, Scotland, Ireland and Britain's North American colonies. These movements were the beginnings of evangelicalism. . . . They grew out of the Protestant Reformation as it had been experienced in the British Isles."[1] A few of the highlights may be noted. In 1734 and 1735, a movement sparked by the preaching of Jonathan Edwards, from Northampton, Massachusetts, began to spread across the American colonies. Edwards was a profoundly intellectual clergyman steeped in Puritan thought, and the movement would become known as "The Great Awakening." At Oxford University in 1735, a young George Whitefield, also Calvinist in theology, had experienced a profound conversion and shortly entered upon a lifetime of preaching in both Britain and the American colonies. In 1738, brothers Charles and John Wesley, both deeply influenced by their encounters with Moravian missionaries, each experienced deep personal conversions to Christ. By the following year, John, the founder of the Methodist movement, had begun preaching in the open air (since Anglican churches were closed to him), calling for listeners to repent and accept Christ.[2] This movement may accurately be referred to as *historic* evangelicalism, the font to which all of today's myriad varieties of evangelicalism may be traced.

Difficulties in Defining Evangelicalism

There have been numerous attempts to define evangelicalism. These attempts have been complicated by three factors in particular.

First, evangelicalism has never been static. It has changed over time and continues to change.

Second, evangelicalism has never been confined to one particular denomination. While some denominations are clearly evangelical, in many cases there are large evangelical wings within denominations that are otherwise not evangelical. In general, ecclesiology—a clear doctrine about the nature of the church—has not been a major concern for evangelicals.

Third, and perhaps most important, evangelicals have differed (and frequently splintered) on a wide variety of issues. From the outset, some evangelicals, like the Wesleys, were Arminian, and others like Edwards and Whitefield were Calvinist. Beginning in the early nineteenth century, there were disagreements about the precise nature of Scripture's inspiration, as some evangelicals, particularly in the United States, began to insist that it was essential to affirm the "inerrancy of the original manuscripts" and the "plenary verbal inspiration" of the Bible. There were also differences over how to interpret the Bible. Some evangelicals demanded a strictly literal interpretation, while others saw the importance of recognizing the different genres of literature within the Bible. Evangelicals also differed about eschatology, the role of women (particularly in terms of church leadership), and the relationship of faith and science. This latter was a particularly intense debate in the United States with respect to the theory of evolution and its place in public school curricula.

Evangelicals disagreed about the appropriate style of worship, with some preferring a more structured approach and others regarding almost any advance planning as "stifling the Holy Spirit." There were—and are—significant disagreements about both the means and timing of conversion. For instance, the American evangelist Charles Finney saw conversion to a large degree as a matter of employing the proper technique. Others regarded this as manipulative and a virtual denial of the need for the Holy Spirit's involvement in conversion. Did genuine conversion always mean an instantaneous (and frequently highly emotional) change that could be precisely documented and dated? Many evangelicals believed this to be the case. Others however believed it was perfectly valid for a person to come to real faith gradually and with little emotion.

Evangelicals parted ways over how to respond to the social gospel movement. Some saw it as a distraction from the urgent and sole responsibility of calling hell-bound sinners to repentance and faith. Others pointed to the repeated injunctions in Scripture to provide for the poor and sick and wanted a more holistic approach. The ecumenical movement similarly divided evangelicals, with some regarding efforts toward greater unity (especially if Roman Catholics were involved) as a failure to heed the injunction to "come out from them, and be separate from them, and touch nothing unclean" (2 Cor 6:17). Others, however, pointed to the prayer of Jesus "that they may be one" (John 17:22) as justification for working toward greater cooperation among believers.

Some evangelicals regard dancing; drinking of tea, coffee, and especially alcohol; the use of makeup and lipstick; and attending cinema or theatre as entirely inappropriate. Others disagree. While some evangelicals forbid their children from participation in any kind of recreation or sport on Sundays, even outside of times set for worship services, others are of the opinion that these are healthy and worthy activities for the young once corporate worship is completed.

Today, many evangelicals regard the establishment of the modern state of Israel in 1948 as the fulfillment of biblical prophecy and evidence of the closeness of the second coming of Jesus. These evangelicals frequently voice unquestioning support for Israel. Other evangelicals, usually holding to a different eschatology, see this event as of little or no importance. They point to the frequent denunciations of ancient Israel for economic and social injustice by the Old Testament prophets and argue that modern

Israel's treatment of the Palestinians falls under the same judgement. In a similar fashion, some evangelicals see little point in concerning themselves with environmental issues. If the world is about to be destroyed anyway, why bother? Other evangelicals contend that, regardless of the eventual fate of the planet, Scripture calls humans to be wise caretakers of God's world.

The Common Core of Evangelicalism

With such diverse origins and widespread differences, one can see how fraught is any attempt to define what "evangelical" means. Despite the difficulties, there is in fact a distinct evangelical identity. "[T]here *are*," as D. W. Bebbington, the prominent British church historian notes, "common features that have lasted from the first half of the eighteenth century to the twentieth. It is this continuing set of characteristics that reveals the existence of an Evangelical tradition."[3] Mark Noll concurs, writing, "evangelicalism designates a consistent pattern of convictions and attitudes that have been maintained over the centuries since the 1730s."[4]

Timothy Larsen of Wheaton College points out that any definition requires a context. Evangelicalism did not just suddenly appear on the scene in the early eighteenth century! It grew out of something, or rather a number of somethings. "Evangelicals" he points out, "are a subset within historic, orthodox Christianity."[5] Evangelicals are orthodox Christians and specifically Protestant Christians. As orthodox Christians, evangelicals affirm the historic doctrines of the Trinity and the incarnation as reflected in the Councils of Nicaea and Constantinople.[6] As Protestant Christians, evangelicals affirm the four distinguishing marks of Protestantism: *sola Scriptura* (Scripture alone as the final authority in matters of faith and practice), *sola gratia* (salvation by grace alone), *sola fide* (grace received by faith alone, which itself is also a gift of grace), and *solus Christus* (Christ alone is the mediator between God and humanity).

It is within this context of being orthodox Christians, and specifically Protestant Christians, that we can turn to the most widely accepted definition of evangelicalism,[7] that set out by Bebbington in his seminal work, *Evangelicalism in Modern Britain: A History from the 1730s to the 1980s*. Bebbington lists four specific characteristics or emphases of evangelicals:

> These are the four qualities that have been the special marks of Evangelical religion: *conversionism*, the belief that lives need to be changed, *activism*, the expression of the gospel in effort; *biblicism*, a particular regard for the Bible; and what may be called *crucicentrism*, a stress on

the sacrifice of Christ on the cross. Together they form a quadrilateral of priorities that is the basis of Evangelicalism.[8]

Although acknowledging that "[v]ariations there have certainly been," Bebbington insists, "[t]here is nevertheless a common core that has remained remarkably constant down the centuries."[9] These four characteristics "have formed a permanent deposit of faith."[10]

Given their widespread acceptance as an accurate way of describing evangelicalism, we will use Bebbington's four terms to explore the theological convictions distinct to evangelicals. If our goal is to formulate principles for truly evangelical worship, we must first understand these distinctive evangelical theological convictions.

Conversionism

Central to evangelicalism was the conviction that all human beings, being estranged from God as a result of sin, were justly subject to divine judgement that would result in eternal death. Instead of experiencing the abundant life that God intended—life with purpose, meaning, wholeness, and joy—our lives apart from God were "cabined, cribbed, confined," smaller not larger, lacking in meaning and purpose, incomplete and sad. The good news was that God had already been working across millennia to restore and renew God's estranged and broken creation. Acting out of love, God had provided a means for sin to be forgiven, estrangement ended, and right relationship restored. In amazing love and grace, God had, in Jesus Christ, become fully human. By his life, death, and resurrection, Jesus had made salvation possible: salvation *from* eternal death, the permanently shriveled and meaningless life apart from God; salvation *from* self-absorption and self-preoccupation; salvation *for* entering life more joyfully, for love of God and others.[11]

Regardless of whether emphasis sometimes fell (overly heavily at times) on the danger of damnation and the torment awaiting in hell, or on the joy and wholeness to which God through Christ invited humanity, evangelicals constantly urged people "to turn away from their sins in repentance and to Christ in faith."[12]

This emphasis on the need for conversion is seen in the preaching of the earliest evangelicals. In his famous sermon, "Sinners in the Hands of an Angry God," preached in Enfield, Connecticut, in summer 1741, Jonathan Edwards told his listeners that his intention was "to wake up the unconverted people in this congregation."[13] Emphasizing the uncertainty of life, which might end at any moment, and the eternal torments of the damned, Edwards insisted, "Now you have an extraordinary opportunity. This day Christ has thrown the door of mercy wide open and stands crying with a loud voice to poor sinners."[14] His sermon, which had members of the congregation weeping, moaning, and desperately asking how they could be saved, drew to its conclusion saying, "Now let everyone who is still without Christ and hanging over the pit . . . answer to the loud calls . . . let everyone who is without Christ now wake up and flee from the wrath to come."[15] In "The Way to the Kingdom," preached in 1746, John Wesley told his hearers that they needed a lively, trusting faith, not merely intellectual assent:

> Only beware thou do not deceive thy own soul with regard to the nature of this faith. It is not (as some have fondly conceived) a bare assent to the truth of the Bible, of the articles of our creed, or of all that is contained in the Old and New Testament. The devils believe this . . . and yet they are devils still. But it is, over and above this, a sure trust in the mercy of God through Christ Jesus. It is a confidence in a pardoning God. It is a divine evidence of conviction that "God was in Christ, reconciling the world to himself . . . ;" and that I, even I, am now reconciled to God by the blood of the cross. Dost thou thus believe?[16]

Similarly, in what is likely his most famous sermon, "The Almost Christian," preached five years earlier, Wesley warned against the danger of nominal as opposed to genuine Christianity. It was not enough, he warned his listeners at the University Church of St. Mary's in Oxford, to avoid taking the Lord's name in vain, profaning the Sabbath, adultery, fornication, drunkenness, to undertake good works, attend church services frequently, engage in family devotions, or be sincere.[17] Rather, "right and true Christian faith is . . . not only to believe the Holy Scripture and the articles of our faith are true, but also to have a sure trust and confidence to be saved from everlasting damnation by Christ."[18] Wesley concluded by urging his listeners, "Awake, then . . . and call upon thy God . . . cry unto him day and night . . . until thou knowest in whom thou hast believed, and canst say 'My Lord and My God.'"[19] Despite his sharp theological differences with Wesley, George Whitefield sounded a parallel warning in "Marks of a True Conversion":

> Though we call ourselves Christians and would consider it as an affront put upon us, for anyone to doubt whether we were Christians or not;

yet there are a great many who bear the name of Christ that yet do not so much as know what real Christianity is. Hence it is that if you ask a great many upon what their hopes of heaven are founded, they will tell you that they belong to this or that or the other denomination, and party of Christians, into which Christendom is now unhappily divided. If you ask others upon what foundation they have built their hope of heaven, they will tell you that they have been baptized, that their fathers and mothers presented them to the Lord Jesus Christ in their infancy; and though, instead of fighting under Christ's banner, they have been fighting against him almost ever since they were baptized, yet because they have been admitted to church, and their names are in the register book of the parish, therefore they will make us believe that their names are also written in the Book of Life . . . . a great many . . . are what we call "negatively good people" . . . . they live so as their neighbours cannot say that they do anybody harm . . . . [Others are] what the world calls an "honest moral man," if he does justly . . . is now and then good natured, reaches out his hand to the poor, receives the Sacrament once or twice a year, and is outwardly sober and honest.[20]

But none of this was sufficient for salvation. These folk might have "Christ in their heads [but] they have not Christ in their hearts."[21] What was needed was genuine faith, which was not to be thought of as something conjured up in oneself, for that would make it a human work, but rather it was God's gift.[22] Rather "faith is the instrument whereby the sinner applies . . . the redemption of Jesus Christ to his heart. And to whomsoever God gives such a faith (for it is a free gift of God), he may lift up his head with boldness; he need not fear . . . he is passed from death to life."[23] To those whom Whitefield hoped had through his preaching become convinced that the care of their souls was the one thing most needed, he urged, "let the conviction work, let it drive you immediately to the throne of grace."[24]

For evangelicals the stark choice was life or death, heaven or hell, Christ's abundance or Satan's scarcity. It was therefore a primary responsibility to urge all people to choose rightly by means of repentance from sin and genuine faith in Christ.

Activism

Evangelicals also considered that it was both a virtue and a responsibility to be busy in the world. It is no accident that hymns such as "Work for the Night Is Coming," "A Charge to Keep I Have," "Rescue the Perishing," "I'll Go Where You Want Me to Go," "We've a Story to Tell to the Nations,"

"Forth in Thy Name, O Lord I Go, My Daily Labor to Pursue," and many others that reflected this insistence on active Christianity were favourites in evangelical hymnody.

This activism could be expressed in various ways, but two stand out in particular: evangelism/mission and social reform.

Not surprisingly, work aimed at inviting others to repentance and faith was highly regarded. Evangelistic preaching was a primary means of undertaking this task. But the urgent need for conversion led evangelicals to evangelistic activity on many fronts. Tract societies proliferated. The British and Foreign Bible Society, established in 1804 with a mission to make the Bible available to every person in a language they could understand, had distinctly evangelical origins and was soon followed by the founding of the American Bible Society in 1816. Evangelical convictions led Baptist cobbler William Carey to become the founder of the modern Protestant missionary movement. By the nineteenth century, countless missionary societies, frequently cross-denominational in nature, were supporting thousands of missionaries around the world. Sunday school children were regaled with tales of heroic missionaries such as Carey, Adoniram Judson, David Livingstone, Lottie Moon, and Hudson Taylor.

Evangelical activism also extended toward social reform. Evangelicals critiqued what they saw as societal evils and worked to bring society into closer alignment with the teachings of Jesus. John Howard (1726–1790), a tireless advocate for reform of the often horrendous conditions of prisons, visited and reported on hundreds of prisons in Great Britain and continental Europe. Education was also an important evangelical cause. Hannah More (1745–1833), playwright, author of numerous evangelical tracts, and philanthropist, had despite serious opposition established at least a dozen schools for children by the time of her death. Similarly, Robert Raikes (1736–1811) is credited as the founder of the Sunday school movement. Raikes saw schooling as a measure for preventing boys from the slums becoming involved in crime. His schools, run by laypeople who used the Bible as a textbook, taught reading, something unavailable otherwise, since most city dwelling boys worked six days a week in factories. Despite criticism that the schools were a violation of the commandment forbidding work on the Sabbath, the schools prospered and were educating hundreds of thousands of children by the time Raikes died. The appalling conditions in factories and mines also received evangelical attention. Anthony Ashley-Cooper, seventh Earl of Shaftesbury, a self-professed evangelical who became known as "the poor man's Earl," saw his calling as labouring among and for the poor. Consequently, he led campaigns that resulted in banning the employment of young children from work in factories, the establishment of a maximum ten-hour workday, ending the employment of women and of girls and boys under ten from working in coal mines, and eliminating the use of child chimney sweeps. He also worked tirelessly to improve the abysmal conditions of insane asylums and the treatment of the insane. William Wilberforce (1759–1833), who had experienced a profound evangelical conversion, championed a wide variety of causes. He founded the Society for the Prevention of Cruelty for Animals, led a campaign that forced the British East India Company to lift restrictions on missionaries in India, and criticized the British there for racial prejudice and failing to put an end to practices such as infanticide and suttee. Most notable, however, Wilberforce advocated tirelessly for the abolition of slavery in the British Empire. In this he was supported by his friend and former slave trader John Newton (1725–1807), who had become a prominent evangelical Anglican clergyman. Wilberforce died just three days after learning that passage of the Slavery Abolition Act was certain.

Biblicism

Although an emphasis on the decisive authority and sufficiency of Scripture in matters of faith and practice—*sola Scriptura*—is common to all Protestant Christians, from the outset evangelicals have been particularly noted for their high view of the authority of Scripture and intense devotion to it. Hence, Bebbington contends that "The third main feature of the Evangelicals, their devotion to the Bible, has been the result of their belief that all spiritual truth is to be found in its pages."[25] For evangelicals, the Bible trumped all other authorities, including (some might say especially!) church officials and church tradition. The Bible and the Bible alone was the final authority in all matters of faith and practice. Evangelicals also "have tended to follow the Reformers' principles" when it came to interpreting Scripture: "that, first the authoritative sense is the literal sense, and second, Scripture interprets [and never contradicts] Scripture."[26]

This commitment was (and is) reflected not only in efforts both to translate the Bible into virtually every one of the world's languages and then to distribute it but also in widespread devotional practices that were (and are) encouraged by evangelical clergy. Seemingly innumerable devotional books and plans for reading through the Bible poured from evangelical pens. John Wesley required that all Methodists be engaged in daily, personal reading of the Bible. George Whitefield similarly insisted that it was the duty of every individual to study the Scriptures. Today's "quiet time"—a term used by many evangelicals to refer to a daily period set aside for private prayer and reading Scripture—is clearly a descendant of these early evangelical practices. Evidence of evangelical biblicism can also be seen in many contemporary choruses that are, essentially, paraphrases of Scripture, in the publication of numerous commentaries, an astonishing variety of Bible study groups (for men, women, teenagers, university students, retirees, dieters, alcoholics, new mothers, physicians, nurses, college faculty members, police officers, firefighters, seafarers), and the heavy emphasis on biblical studies in many evangelical colleges and seminaries.

None of this is to suggest that there have not been differences among evangelicals about the precise nature of the authority of Scripture. There have been and continue to be differences, and they have been especially problematic in the United States. In the nineteenth century, some American evangelicals, notably those of the "Princeton school," developed and promoted a theology that saw the Bible, in the original autographs, as inerrant in all matters whatever—scientific, historical, and geographical—as well as in matters pertaining to faith and practice. Some even argued, inaccurately, that this had been the view of the Protestant Reformers, or even of the early church. Other evangelicals, however, while holding the Bible in equal esteem, took the position that Scripture was authoritative only in matters of faith and practice. These differences have often led to heated disagreements that have became famous (or infamous) in evangelical circles, even in recent times. For example, as Fuller Theological Seminary moved from having a statement of faith that insisted on inerrancy in all matters whatever to a statement that instead referred to Scripture as being authoritative in matters of faith and practice, an enormous row erupted that pitted inerrantists such as Harold Lindsell, who authored *The Battle for the Bible*, against other equally evangelical faculty members such as David Hubbard and George Ladd. In the Southern Baptist Convention, differences about Scripture eventually led in the late twentieth and early twenty-first centuries to a highly politicized atmosphere and a painful fracturing of the denomination as many non-inerrantist evangelicals left or were forced out.[27]

Despite these and other disagreements about the precise nature of the authority of Scripture and its interpretation, there is clearly an identifiable evangelical "tradition." At a minimum, this tradition affirms the authority and sufficiency of the Bible in matters of faith and practice, and it interprets the text of Scripture in a manner that is clearly indebted to the Protestant Reformers.

Cruicentrism

Evangelicals were historically focused on the cross of Christ and what was happening during the crucifixion—in theological terminology, the atonement. For evangelicals this was and remains of central importance. However they explained it, evangelicals believed that in dying on the cross, Jesus was reconciling humanity and God, who were estranged as a result of human sin. Christ's death was the ultimate demonstration of God's love toward fallen humanity, without which no reconciliation would have been possible. Like the Protestant Reformers, evangelicals insisted that salvation was solely the gift of God's grace (*sola gratia*), appropriated solely by faith (*sola fide*) in Christ and his atoning work on the cross.

Evangelicals did differ on precisely how the reconciliation Jesus accomplished by his death should be described. Bebbington notes, "The standard view of Evangelicals was that Christ died as a substitute for sinful mankind. Human beings, they held, were so rebellious against God that a just penalty would have been death."[28] The imagery here is that of a law court, which sees the work of Jesus in largely judicial terms, with Christ fulfilling the requirements of God's law that fallen humanity could not meet. This understanding draws heavily on the book of Hebrews, which sees Jesus as the final and perfect sacrifice. Jesus puts an end to the need for the animal sacrifices of the Old Testament that foreshadowed his self-sacrifice. It would not be overstating the case to say that in many evangelical circles this explanation, attributed primarily to Augustine (d. 430) and Anselm (d. 1109), is regarded as *the only* valid understanding of the atonement. However, as Bebbington also observes, although the most common view of the atonement was that of penal substitution, this was by no means universal.[29]

In recent years, some evangelicals have argued that there are several images of the atonement given in the Bible and the view that the innocent Jesus Christ died in our place—penal substitution—is but one of these.[30] Others, concerned that Anselm's view attributes violence to God's nature and thus validates violence, or that Anselm's theory resembles a sort of divine child abuse, have expressed serious doubts about, entirely rejected, or significantly nuanced his explanation.[31]

Regardless of their differing understandings, evangelicals have consistently agreed that the death of Jesus on the cross was essential to the reconciliation of God and humanity. Consequently, for evangelical theology, spirituality, preaching, and hymnody,[32] the cross was and remains central.

Principles of Evangelical Common Worship

It may seem obvious to some, but it needs to be said emphatically: evangelical common worship should be formed, shaped, driven, and based on our distinctive theological convictions. Otherwise our worship becomes either not clearly evangelical—failing to hold and express evangelical convictions—or, if shaped by the wider culture instead of core evangelical theological principles, it becomes markedly secular.

Careful reflection about the distinctive theological traits of historic evangelicalism will help us establish principles for common worship that is truly evangelical in nature. If we are to remain faithful to what evangelicals stood for historically, that faithfulness must be reflected in our common worship. We will reflect, then, in turn, on each of the distinctive evangelical traits just outlined in order to determine what common worship among evangelicals should look like and how it should be shaped and formed in ways that are faithful to our theological heritage.

Conversionism and Common Worship

From the outset, as we have seen, evangelicals have emphasized the need for personal repentance and acceptance of Jesus as Lord. Many thoughtful evangelicals contend that this important emphasis has been badly misunderstood in terms of how it applies to common worship. Put bluntly, none of the four "circles" of worship, including common worship, is evangelism. Worship, as we have already seen "*is never meant to serve any other purpose except the glory of God. The end of worship is worship*" (my emphasis).[33] Worship is about praising and adoring God. Whenever the focus of worship is on *anything* other than God, however worthy and important that thing may be—and evangelism is both—then worship is secularized, for God is being moved away from the centre. Evangelism certainly can and should be a byproduct of genuine common worship. It is not, however, the worship itself.

There is little evidence that the early church saw common worship as a means of evangelism.[34] Certainly the book of Acts does not leave one with the impression that the first followers of Jesus regarded evangelism as something that was the responsibility of the clergy during Sunday worship! Instead, it was to be both the responsibility and joy of *every* follower of Jesus. In this attitude, those first Christians were following the Great Commission as it is recorded in Matthew's Gospel. It is important to pay careful attention to both the words and their order in this text. First we are told that the disciples worship Jesus (Matt 28:17). *Then*, Jesus commissions his followers, "Go therefore and make disciples . . ." (Matt 28:19a). The worship *leads* to evangelism. Here, in nascent form, is the New Testament's pattern: common worship results in evangelism *in daily life*. Out of the experience of common worship—taught, instructed, trained, encouraged, and equipped—Christians return to the wider world outside the church walls, commissioned to build deep relationships with other people, relationships that will allow us to speak about the one who is central to our lives and invite others to repentance and faith. "[E]vangelism," as Marva Dawn succinctly puts it, "[is] . . . an outgrowth of worship."[35] Common worship is for the committed followers of Jesus Christ. Evangelism is for those who are not believers.

If the evangelical emphasis on the importance of conversion has misled us into confusing common worship and evangelism, that in turn has also led to other significant theological problems. First, it has resulted in a general "dumbing down" of common worship. If common worship is the primary means by which to reach people with the gospel, then, so the thinking goes, we must make Sunday worship more "accessible" and "attractive" to those who know little or nothing about Jesus Christ. Consequently, in an effort to make common worship more attractive, the harder bits of the gospel, particularly the demands of a sovereign God on our lives, are often downplayed. We sing a lot of "What a Friend We Have in Jesus" and not much of "Holy, Holy, Holy! Lord God Almighty!" But

> to express dissatisfaction with a service because it does not communicate the Christian faith to contemporary man [*sic*] is to miss the point of what Christian worship essentially is, the offering to God of that honor, praise, thanksgiving, and obedience of which one who has already experienced true Christian faith is totally convinced He is worthy.[36]

Second, confusing common worship with evangelism frequently means that laypeople do not see themselves as responsible for evangelism. How ironic and tragic given that evangelism is so important for evangelicals! Sadly, evangelism has often come to be seen as something to be done on Sunday mornings by the minister. She or he is regarded as primarily or even solely responsible for the church's outreach. This stands in stark contrast to the conviction that the Great Commission applies to *every* Christian of *every* generation. It is, moreover, a denial of the biblical insistence on the priesthood of *all* believers, that *all* followers of Jesus are called to be priests, building bridges between God and estranged humanity. Third, seeing common worship as evangelism often results in a near total lack of formation or discipleship. If every sermon and every worship service must be focused on the call for conversion, there is precious little time left for teaching people what they should do or how they should live *after* they have committed their lives to Christ. Is it any wonder that many people in the pews feel themselves ill equipped to speak about their faith to others when they have rarely heard a sermon about anything other than how to become a Christian?

Indeed, fourth, one can argue that confusing worship and evangelism tends in general toward blunting or significantly reducing *all* "by-products" of common worship. For example, such confusion allows little time for deep teaching that challenges God's people to be and act as a countercultural minority. How can there be mutual encouragement in living out this countercultural life when nothing other than the initial step of becoming a follower of Jesus is ever addressed? Can deep community be built solely around the experience of becoming a Christian, without reference to what follows—the trials, temptations, and joys of following Jesus? How am I to learn what it means to be salt and light from Monday to Saturday if on Sunday all I hear is the importance of becoming a Christian and how to do so? None of this means there are *never* occasions when a common worship service should have a sermon that invites listeners to repentance and to confession of Christ's lordship. But these occasions should be fairly rare and planned to align with those few Sundays a year when one might reasonably expect a number of nonbelievers to be present.

Besides the theological problems, the confusion of common worship with evangelism has one major practical problem to which we have already made reference. In a secular society, treating common worship as a way to do evangelism is almost entirely irrelevant. By definition, secular people are rarely, if ever, present for Sunday morning worship. To imagine that common worship is a highly effective vehicle for outreach, witness, or evangelism is nonsense. The secular people who need to repent of sin and confess Christ as Lord are not sitting in the pews on most Sunday mornings. They are still at home in bed or having brunch at a favourite restaurant or getting ready to take their children to hockey, soccer, or baseball practice. To see common worship as evangelism means, at least on the vast majority of Sundays, literally preaching to the converted.

Rather than expecting secular people to cross cultural boundaries so that the evangelism can happen inside the church building where we are comfortable, common worship should send us out into the world, to places, activities, and situations where we may meet and build genuine relationships with those who are not Christians. That is precisely what Whitefield and the Wesleys did when they began speaking outdoors—instead of expecting the unchurched to come to them inside church buildings. The attractional approach to evangelism—"if we can just get them in the door of the church"—stems from the Christendom model when the church held a privileged place in society, everyone was under social or family or even legal pressure to attend Sunday worship services, and there was little else to do on that day. But Christendom is gone, and this approach to evangelism needs to go with it.

Let there be no confusion: common worship that is genuinely evangelical will always regard "conversionism" as important. But if it is to be theologically responsible and faithful to Scripture, not to mention culturally relevant, our common worship must see evangelism, outreach, mission, and witness as *by-products* of worship that should happen *outside of and as a result of* common worship. The gathering on Sunday morning is for committed Christians—that they may go back out into the world to witness to Christ by word and deed.

In practical terms, what might all this mean? Distinctively evangelical common worship—especially the preaching component—will encourage *all* believers to engage in witness beyond the four walls of the church on Sunday mornings. Evangelical preaching will *equip* followers of Jesus to do just this, through teaching that deeply shapes people in a biblical worldview, wrestles with criticisms and questions from a secular culture, and emphasizes the joy and wholeness, purpose and meaning to which God lovingly invites humanity (as opposed to an emphasis on fleeing judgement). What if bulletins were used as teaching tools? Instead of cute quips, cheesy quotations and cartoons, and sentimental poetry, how about the occasional book or movie review, reflecting on what a book or movie tells us about our culture, the angsts that dominate it, and the questions it has? As opposed to the "altar call," perhaps every Sunday worship service should include a "commissioning" whereby worshippers are charged and reminded each week that they are *sent* out into the wider world to bear witness to Jesus by their words and actions.

Activism and Common Worship

Evangelicals are distinguished by a conviction that weighs heavily, that we are called to be actively about the work of the Kingdom, Christ's business, in the world. As Mark Noll writes, "the foundation [of evangelicalism] was unswerving belief in the need for conversion (the new birth) *and the necessity of a life of active holiness.*"[37]

This activism may be broadly and somewhat artificially divided into two parts: evangelism and social action. What is critical is that neither of these are seen in Scripture as primarily taking place *as part of common worship*. Rather, they are chiefly *responses* to the experience of meeting with God during common worship, responses that happen *after* common worship is concluded.

In common worship we (hopefully) encounter God and begin to see the world from God's perspective. From that perspective of unconditional, unchanging love, we see the need of those whose lives, having no lively faith in Jesus, are anything but "abundant." Instead they are dogged by an often unspoken, even inarticulate fear that life has no point, meaning, or purpose. Estranged from God, such folk have often experienced estrangement from other people and the wider creation as well. They are in danger of a pointless, meaningless, purposeless, estranged eternity. We respond by speaking to those in this situation of what we experienced when we decided to accept Jesus as Lord. As evangelicals we may also respond by enabling others to go to foreign lands to make Christ known, and by supporting efforts to translate and distribute Scripture. Looking at the world from God's perspective, we are no longer able to ignore the hunger, injustice, pain, suffering, and political and economic corruption in the world. We respond both by meeting the immediate needs *and* through a serious engagement with our culture—which will often mean challenging widely accepted social, economic, and political practices.

What does this mean for Sunday morning worship? Genuinely evangelical common worship will result in active response, *but* most of that response will take place from Monday to Saturday, outside the walls of the church building. Common worship can and should point to and encourage that response. This would seem to raise questions about some typical practices of evangelical worship. For example, is it appropriate to have the offering early or midway through the worship service? What does the offering mean? If giving money is an act of response to my meeting God, doesn't the offering belong toward the end of the worship service? What about the prayers of the people (sometimes called the "pastoral prayer")? Shouldn't this be a response to God's perspective on the world—a response in which we pray for the spiritual as well as physical and emotional needs of the world? And if a response, should it not occur *after* I have heard God's word read and preached? How about the concluding elements of the worship service? Is there an actual commissioning of some sort—am I being sent out into the new week to bear witness to Jesus *and* alleviate suffering? Is the benediction an actual blessing—rather than a "closing prayer"—that sends me out into the world to do God's work, assured of God's presence, love, and peace?

Biblicism and Common Worship

Although differing on the precise details of the nature of Scripture's inspiration, evangelicals have consistently held a high view of the authority of Scripture. From the outset they believed that it was the final authority in matters of faith and practice, the supreme guide, central to all of daily living. Three practices for common worship can be immediately derived from this understanding of Scripture.

First, Scripture should have a prominent, critical, and central place in every service of evangelical common worship. Sadly, this is not the case in many evangelical churches in Canada and the United States. Many congregations that would vehemently claim to be "Bible believing" actually give little time to reading Scripture on most Sundays. In many cases the norm is that only two or three verses of Scripture are read, and these are almost invariably from the New Testament. It is extremely strange that churches that are both heirs of the Protestant Reformation and evangelical read *far less* Scripture on any given Sunday than will be read in every Roman Catholic parish in the world on that day. Is the widespread lack of personal knowledge of Scripture in the pews partly attributable to the lack of Scripture reading during common worship? James F. White writes, "[W]e must realize the *centrality of scripture*—all of scripture," and he insists the days are gone "when we could be content with a few verses read as a sermon text. God's word speaks for itself."[38] Indeed, I would argue that the evangelical principle of a high view of the authority of Scripture means that evangelical common worship should be permeated by and soaked in Scripture. Not only should there be extended reading of Scripture prior to the sermon, but Scripture should be employed in other elements of worship services as well, such as calls to worship, assurances of pardon, prayers, and benedictions. Some contemporary worship songs that are close paraphrases of Scripture as well as the traditional psalter set to music[39] may also serve to immerse common worship in the words and worldview of the Bible.

Second, a high view of Scripture means evangelical common worship must be shaped and defined by Scripture (and Scripture's reasons for worship—not the culture's reasons). Evangelicals should want to "chain their worship to Scripture itself,"[40] and Scripture makes it clear that worship is *not* about whatever happens to please, stimulate, or attract *us*. Worship, according to Scripture, isn't about *us*—it's about God. Worship, according to Scripture, is to be God-centred and, more specifically, Christ-centred, since we worship the God whom we have come to know best in Jesus. To be faithful to the evangelical heritage of a high view of Scripture means constantly seeking to worship in such a manner as will please *God*, as *God* has revealed this to us in Scripture. We want *every* aspect of common worship—content, style, music—to jibe with Scripture. We must not accept "the prevailing assumption that how we worship is simply a matter of style, not substance."[41] Genuinely evangelical worship understands that *God* takes worship with the utmost seriousness. According to Scripture, God *does not* regard anything and everything to be acceptable worship. *Not* everything goes. Consider how much of the Torah, especially Leviticus, is devoted to the most detailed instructions about worship! Michael Horton points out that "Aaron's sons, Nadab and Abihu, served the Lord as temple priests, but when they offered a sacrifice that God had not commanded, God struck them dead. . . . They presumed to serve God in the way they found 'worshipful,' but they were unwilling to regard God's commanded worship as sufficient."[42]

Let us be clear indeed about this: "God . . . does not leave the matter of how we approach him in our hands."[43] We need to remember that "there are clearly required elements that God has commanded for his worship. While one cannot point to a single liturgy and say that it contains the only form of genuine worship, some are clearly better than others in being faithful to God's regulation of his worship, which he has always taken very seriously."[44] Michael Horton pulls no punches when he observes,

> In some Christian circles today, one actually hears comments such as, "I don't like church A because there's no life. It's way too heavy and overpowering. It's not heartfelt worship." It is quite possible, of course, that each of these accusations means exactly what it says. . . . But it is often the case that "life . . ." means a concert-like atmosphere in which volume, staging, and lighting play an enormous role. "Heavy" and "overpowering" mean that there is a sense of transcendence that is unfamiliar in our experience as a secularized people. . . . If we are worshiping the God of Abraham and Jesus, the style of that worship will necessarily be "weighty" or "heavy."[45]

Third, a high view of the authority of Scripture, what Bebbington calls "biblicism," historically led to placing high value on preaching, particularly expository and doctrinal preaching. Indeed, "[s]o important is this emphasis [on preaching] that many accounts of evangelicalism are essentially a history of evangelical preachers."[46] In practice this emphasis on preaching meant that "the sermon often dominated the liturgy."[47] Evangelicals believed that preaching was to be tied solidly to Scripture. This resulted in a heavy focus on expository preaching. Traditionally, a pulpit was one of the central pieces of furniture in Protestant churches in general and evangelical churches in particular. Very often a large Bible rested on the pulpit. Sometimes the Bible was physically carried into the sanctuary in front of the minister and placed on the pulpit at the beginning of each worship service. This visually conveyed the message that when someone spoke from the pulpit, he or she spoke with authority *only* insofar as he or she *spoke out of Scripture*. Historically, pulpits were often quite large, elaborate affairs—the preacher was symbolically engulfed, surrounded by the word. By contrast, what message is conveyed in many evangelical churches today where, if there is a pulpit at all, it is often a small Plexiglas lectern, dwarfed by myriads of electronic equipment? Does this suggest that preaching is central to what is happening? Does it suggest that preaching is tied to Scripture? This miniaturizing of pulpits is not just nitpicking. The organization of sacred space reflects a theological trend that simply does not align with the historic evangelical understanding of preaching. Michael Horton comments, "While evangelicals . . . hold to a high doctrine of Scripture in principle, the last . . . decades have . . . seen a growing disregard for making their sermons expositions of Scripture; rather it's often the case that the Bible is used as a sourcebook of quotations for what *we* really want to say."[48]

Often, he continues, "It seems that very little serious exegesis is done in sermons today, and that can only encourage a subtle but effective process of secularizing our churches in the very act of 'preaching.'"[49] Instead of being expository or doctrinal in nature, a good deal of preaching in evangelical churches is focused on problems of family, relationships, health, or finances. It is not that such subjects do not need to be addressed. But historically, evangelicals understood that the movement should primarily be from God and God's word *to* these problems, not the other way around. Scripture, God's word to his people, was to control the agenda, *not* our problems or issues. Evangelicals understood that the goal was life reordered according to God's will as revealed in Scripture, *not* that Scripture proves helpful in dispensing useful advice and tips for managing to cope.

Crucicentrism and Common Worship

The emphasis on the cross and the atonement in evangelical theology points to two important practical principles for worship that is authentically evangelical.

First, that God had to go the extreme of the cross in order to rescue humanity allows no room for any notions that humans can—with just a little divine help—improve themselves and set to rights their broken relationship with God. If such a notion is conveyed in any aspect of common worship, particularly preaching, we are once again seeing secularization, for the focus is on humanity with God at the edges, brought in when and if necessary. The cross confronts us with our total inability to justify ourselves before God. Deriving from our Protestant roots, the evangelical focus on the cross requires that we have what Martin Luther called a "theology of the cross," as opposed to a "theology of glory." What is the difference? A theology of the cross insists that while it may seem foolish to the world at large, our salvation, rescue, wholeness, purpose, and joy depend *entirely* on the work of Christ on the cross (1 Cor 1:18-25). A theology of glory sees the ways of God as generally understandable by human reason; a theology of the cross is much more humble. It knows that God's ways are often mysterious and paradoxical in nature. A theology of glory emphasizes human effort while a theology of the cross, consistent with the parable of Jesus, insists that even if we were to do all that we should, we would still be "unprofitable servants; we have done [only] that which was our duty to do" (Luke 17:10, AV). A theology of glory tends to minimize, downgrade, or ignore painful and difficult things, to move past them quickly and focus on "success," while a theology of the cross names and acknowledges sin, suffering, and failure. (Perhaps this is why many evangelicals prefer to skip directly from Palm Sunday to Easter Sunday, and why many evangelical worship services on Good Friday are not solemn, somber reflections on the cross but early celebrations of the resurrection!)

A theology of glory finds it difficult to see much of God's hand in the life of a person who is "unsuccessful." Indeed, preachers operating out of a theology of glory may well tell the person experiencing divorce, bankruptcy, unemployment, or poor health that the problem is a lack of faith on their part. A theology of the cross, on the other hand, believes that God is often to be found in the wreckage of our lives, our doubts, brokenness, failed relationships, and sin, because in those circumstances, instead of imagining we are able to cope, we realize we are not coping, and cry out for God's mercy and grace. All of this means that genuine evangelical theology and evangelical worship, which is focused on the cross, allows no room for understanding the Christian faith primarily as a means of helping us cope with the problems and challenges of daily life or as a way to achieve prosperity, happiness, or good health. This raises serious questions about worship services and sermons that are focused on me, how to improve my family situation, finances, and relationships, as well as the self-absorbed spirituality of some mega churches and their high-profile pastors. What is one to make of churches whose leaders produce books with titles like *Every Day a Friday: How to be Happier 7 Days a Week* and *Your Best Life Now: 7 Steps to Living at Your Full Potential* (Joel Osteen); *Reposition Yourself: Living Life without Limits* and *Breaking the Spirit of Failure* (T. D. Jakes); *Load Up Pocket Devotional: 31 Devotions to Revolutionize Your Future, Prayer: Your Foundation for Success, The Laws of Prosperity*, and *Prosperity: The Choice Is Yours* (Kenneth Copeland)?

A second practical principle for common worship derived from the historic evangelical emphasis on the cross is tied closely to both biblicism and conversionism. Scripture gives more than one way to explain what Jesus was doing on the cross, and we should employ *all* these explanations in order best to present the gospel.

The evangelical commitment to Scripture (biblicism) should result in our seeing that the Bible gives us more than one explanation or description of what was happening that day outside of Jerusalem when Jesus was nailed to a cross. The penal substitution theory is only one explanation. Why should we be surprised? Do we really imagine that *any* description could completely describe what was happening? In *Professing the Faith: Christian Theology in a North American Context,* Canadian theologian Douglas John Hall divides the various historical explanations of the atonement into three groups: theories focused on the idea of rescue, freedom, or liberation;[50] theories characterized by the idea of sacrifice; and theories that emphasize the idea of demonstration or revelation of God's love.[51] Each of these three major types corresponds to a particular period in European history, and each explanation addresses the anxiety that was most widespread in that period.[52]

Closely following Paul Tillich's analysis in *The Courage to Be*,[53] Hall argues that the first of these theories, those focused on rescue or liberation, spoke to the chief angst of people living in the early centuries after Christ in the Roman Empire: oppression and enslavement by supernatural forces of evil, widely believed to be the cause of human misery.[54] Hence rescue or liberation theories emphasized the biblical connections between Moses and Jesus, seeing Jesus as "the greater Moses," the liberator who frees us not from physical slavery in Egypt but from slavery to sin, death, and the devil. This idea is especially prominent in Matthew's Gospel, which draws many parallels between Jesus and Moses, but the idea also appears in the letters of the New Testament (Rom 8:2, 18-22; Gal 1:4; 5:1; 1 Pet 2:16).

The second type of atonement explanation revolved around the idea of sacrifice, and this "came to dominate the Middle Ages of the West, replacing for the most part the earlier theory."[55] The chief angst of society had changed from that of the ancient world. Amid the rubble of the Roman Empire, with one hegemonic church that emphasized the torments awaiting guilty souls who would be judged by a terrifying and vengeful God, in a world where life could be ended by everything from plague and famine to incessant feudal warfare, it is hardly surprising that, for most, the "dominant anxiety" became that of "guilt and condemnation."[56] Nor should it be too surprising that the church found in Scripture an explanation of the atonement that sought to address that anxiety. Hence St. Anselm (1033–1104) argued that God had to become a human being to solve the human problem of sin, because *only* God, by becoming human, could pay the just debt or penalty that divine justice demanded. Sacrificial theories have a deep vein of biblical materials to mine. They link the ritual animal sacrifices of the Old Testament with Jesus as the new and final sacrifice in the New. Jesus becomes, in Hebrews, both the sacrifice and the sacrificer.

The third type of atonement theory is especially associated with Peter Abelard (1097–1142). For Abelard, Christ's suffering and crucifixion was not about satisfying divine justice. Instead, the person who heard this story would be radically changed, moved to a "new consciousness of God's love."[57] This explanation spoke to many people in the late eighteenth through early twentieth centuries. It was a time of unsettling social changes—rapid industrialization, unrestrained laissez-faire capitalism, and increasing urbanization—a time in which hearing of God's astonishing love was sorely needed. This kind of explanation of the atonement can point to the many instances in the Gospels of individuals who were strangely, deeply, and profoundly moved by Jesus—and chose to follow him. Both John's Gospel (John 13:15) and Peter's First Letter (1 Pet 2:21) refer to Jesus as an example or model.

Each of these explanations, not to mention a number of more contemporary explanations, draws from Scripture. As such, evangelicals, committed to a high view of Scripture, should not focus on *only* one explanation of the meaning of the cross—penal substitution—but should draw from *all* the images Scripture provides. If our commitment to Scripture is not sufficient motivation to do this, then surely the evangelical distinctive of "conversionism" should motivate us! We say we are committed to inviting others to follow after Jesus. But the reality is that none of the historic explanations of the meaning of the cross resonate especially well with secular people in Western society. Why? Because they do not speak clearly to the angst that dominates *our* culture. Focusing on only *one* of these historic theories—penal substitution—makes this failure to connect even more pronounced. The fact is that few people in Western society go about daily life concerned about their guilty standing before God, constantly dreading divine judgement. Whether that *is* their situation or not is not the question—the point is that it is not *felt*. What *is* felt—and the chief angst of our society today—is a gnawing fear that there may be no point to it all. Perhaps there is no point to my life, perhaps the universe is merely an immense, cold, uncaring blob in which I am truly alone and without any significance.[58] Our commitment, as evangelicals, to inviting others to join us in following Jesus should move us to careful thought and searching of the Scriptures, in order that we may find ways of saying *how* the cross addresses this angst.

Notes

1. Mark A. Noll, *The Rise of Evangelicalism: The Age of Edwards, Whitefield and the Wesleys*, vol. 1 of A History of Evangelicalism—People, Movements and Ideas in the English-Speaking World (Downers Grove IL: InterVarsity Press, 2003) 18.

2. Not surprisingly, much of the early evangelical movement in the American colonies that would eventually form the United States was initially shaped by and to some degree was derivative of English evangelicalism. For example, one of the primary figures of the First Great Awakening, George Whitefield (1714–1770), was not a native-born American but English, a colleague and friend of the Wesley brothers. Although John Wesley also preached in the United States, more significantly, after the American rebellion, he consecrated Welsh-born, Oxford-educated Thomas Coke (1747–1814) as superintendent—a term quickly replaced by "bishop"—for American Methodists. Francis Asbury (1745–1816), the second American Methodist Bishop, also came from England to the United States and remained there for forty-five years.

3. D. W. Bebbington, *Evangelicalism in Modern Britain: A History from the 1730s to the 1980s* (London: Unwin Hyman, 1989; repr., London: Routledge, 2005) 2, emphasis added.

4. Noll, *Rise of Evangelicalism*, 19.

5. Timothy Larsen, "Defining and locating evangelicalism," in *The Cambridge Companion to Evangelical Theology*, ed. Timothy Larsen, Daniel J. Treier, Cambridge Companions to Religion (Cambridge: Cambridge University Press, 2007) 3.

6. Ibid., 3, 4.

7. American church historian Mark Noll writes, "Many efforts have been made to summarize those convictions and attitudes. One of the most effective is offered by David Bebbington" (Noll, *Rise of Evangelicalism*, 19). The late George Rawlyk, a leading Canadian church historian, also used and regarded as highly persuasive Bebbington's categories. (See, for example, G. A. Rawlyk, *Is Jesus Your Personal Saviour? In Search of Canadian Evangelicalism in the 1990s* [Montreal and Kingston: McGill-Queen's University Press, 1996] 9).

8. Bebbington, *Evangelicalism in Modern Britain*, 2–3.

9. Ibid., 4.

10. Ibid., 271.

11. Douglas John Hall, *Why Christian: For Those on the Edge of Faith* (Minneapolis: Augsburg Fortress, 1998) 38.

12. Bebbington, *Evangelicalism in Modern Britain*, 5.

13. Jonathan Edwards, *Sinners in the Hands of an Angry God*, Made Easier to Read by John Jeffery Fanella (Phillipsburg NJ, Puritan and Reformed Publishing, 1996) 15.

14. Ibid., 26.

15. Ibid., 27, 28.

16. John Wesley, "The Way to the Kingdom," in *John Wesley's Sermons: An Anthology*, ed. Albert C. Outler, Richard P. Heitzenrater (Nashville: Abingdon Press, 1991) 131.

17. Ibid., "The Almost Christian," 63–64.

18. Ibid., 66.

19. Ibid., 68.

20. George Whitefield, "Marks of a True Conversion," in *Sermons of George Whitefield*, ed. Evelyn Bence (Peabody MA: Hendrickson, 2009) 69–70.

21. Ibid., 70.

22. George Whitefield, "What Think Ye of Christ?" in *Sermons of George Whitefield*, ed. Bence, 90.

23. Ibid.

24. George Whitefield, "The Care of the Soul Urged as the One Thing Needful," in *Sermons of George Whitefield*, ed. Bence, 146.

25. Bebbington, *Evangelicalism in Modern Britain*, 12.

26. Kevin J. Vanhooser, "Scripture and Hermeneutics," in *The Oxford Handbook of Evangelical Theology*, ed. Gerald R. McDermott (Oxford: Oxford University Press, 2010) 38.

27. See, for example, Bill J. Leonard, *God's Last and Only Hope: The Fragmentation of the Southern Baptist Convention* (Grand Rapids MI: Eerdmans, 1990); Walter B. Shurden,

Randy Shepley, eds., *Going for the Jugular: A Documentary History of the SBC Holy War* (Macon GA: Mercer University Press, 1996).

28. Bebbington, *Evangelicalism in Modern Britain*, 16.

29. Ibid., 17.

30. See for example James Beilby, Paul R. Eddy, eds., *The Nature of the Atonement: Four Views* (Downers Grove IL: IVP Academic, 2006); Derek Tidball, David Hilborn, Justin Thacker, eds., *The Atonement Debate: Papers from the London Symposium on the Theology of Atonement* (Grand Rapids MI: Zondervan, 2008.)

31. See for example J. Denny Weaver, *The Non-Violent Atonement* (Grand Rapids MI: Eerdmans, 2011); John Sanders, ed. *Atonement and Violence: A Theological Conversation* (Nashville: Abingdon, 2006); Paul S. Fiddes, *Past Event and Present Salvation: The Christian Idea of Atonement* (London: Darton, Longman and Todd, 1989); Paul Fiddes, *The Creative Suffering of God* (Oxford: Clarendon Press, 1992).

32. As is often the case, hymnody reveals what is central to any particular group's theology and spirituality. It should therefore not be a surprise that many of the best-known traditional hymns among evangelicals emphasize the cross. Consider for example this list: "Alas! And Did My Savour Bleed," "Am I a Soldier of the Cross?" "And Can It Be?" "At the Cross," "Are You Washed in the Blood?" "Beneath the Cross of Jesus," "In the Cross of Christ I Glory," "Lift High the Cross," "My Song Is Love Unknown," "Near the Cross," "Nothing But the Blood of Jesus," "Must Jesus Bear the Cross Alone?" "O Sacred Head, Now Wounded," "There Is a Fountain Filled with Blood," "There Is Room at the Cross for You," "The Old Rugged Cross," "The Way of the Cross Leads Home," "Thy Life Was Given for Me," "We Sing the Praise of Him Who Died, of Him who Died Upon the Cross," "When I Survey the Wondrous Cross."

33. Simon Chan, *Liturgical Theology: The Church as Worshiping Community* (Downers Grove IL: InterVarsity Press, 2006) 53.

34. The events on the day of Pentecost (Acts 2) are sometimes cited as an example of worship as evangelism. However, the text says only that the followers of Jesus were "all together in one place" (Acts 2:1), *not* that they were engaged in common worship. Even if one assumes that followers of Jesus were engaged in worship, Peter's evangelistic preaching took place after the sudden end of the common worship and was addressed specifically to those who were *not* part of the church, who had come to investigate the strange phenomena that were happening.

35. Marva J. Dawn, *A Royal "Waste" of Time: The Splendor of Worshiping God and Being Church for the World* (Grand Rapids MI: Eerdmans, 1999) 324.

36. Robert G. Rayburn, *O Come, Let Us Worship: Corporate Worship in the Evangelical Church* (Grand Rapids MI: Baker Book House, 1980; repr., Eugene OR: Wipf and Stock, 2010) 27.

37. Noll, *Rise of Evangelicalism*, 15, emphasis added.

38. James F. White, *Introduction to Christian Worship*, 3rd ed., rev. and exp. (Nashville: Abingdon, 2000) 170.

39. Prior to the Protestant Reformation, while the psalms were often sung during worship services, the singing was limited to clergy and/or choir. The Protestant Reformers believed that all of God's people should be active participants in the worship of God and

that singing was an important part of that worship. Hence, John Calvin supervised the creation of the "Genevan Psalter," the final version of which in 1562 included all 150 psalms set to music. In Scotland, the Scottish Metrical Psalter has been in continuous use among Presbyterians since it was first published in 1650. The *Scottish Metrical Psalter: Psalms of David in Metre* (Point Roberts, Washington, Eremitical Press, 2007) is an inexpensive paperback edition. A useful contemporary psalter, co-published in 2012 by the Calvin Institute of Christian Worship, Faith Alive Christian Resources, and Brazos Press is *Psalms for All Seasons: A Complete Psalter for Worship*. All 150 psalms are set to music—frequently well-known hymns or folk tunes. As well there are appendices providing specific helps for guitar players. For discussions of the value, importance, and use of the psalms in common worship, see Massey H. Shepherd, Jr., *The Psalms in Christian Worship: A Practical Guide* (Minneapolis: Augsburg, 1976); N. T. Wright, *The Case for the Psalms: Why They Are Essential* (San Francisco: HarperOne, 2013).

40. Michael Horton, *A Better Way: Rediscovering the Drama of God-Centered Worship* (Grand Rapids MI: Baker, 2003) 147.

41. Ibid., 11.

42. Ibid.,144.

43. Ibid., 143.

44. Ibid., 142.

45. Ibid., 166.

46. John D. Witvliet, "Worship," in *The Oxford Handbook of Evangelical Theology*, ed. Gerald R. McDermott (Oxford: Oxford University Press, 2010) 316.

47. Ibid., 316, 317.

48. Horton, *A Better Way*, 214.

49. Ibid., 216.

50. Since the publication of Gustaf Aulén's seminal *Christus Victor* in 1931, this explanation of the atonement has been widely accepted as being the "classical" theory prevalent in the early centuries of the church. Aulén also divided theories of the atonement into three broad categories that he called "classical," "objective/Anselmian," and "subjective/humanistic."

51. Douglas John Hall, *Professing the Faith: Christian Theology in a North American Context* (Minneapolis: Fortress Press, 1996) 415.

52. Ibid.

53. Paul Tillich, *The Courage to Be* (New Haven: Yale University Press, 1952).

54. Hall, *Professing the Faith*, 416–17.

55. Ibid., 423.

56. Ibid.

57. Ibid., 430.

58. Contemporary literature as well as theatre, film, art, and music are filled with and clearly reflect this anxiety. For example, in *The Elegance of the Hedgehog* (trans. Alison Anderson [New York: Europa Editions, 2008]), contemporary French philosopher and novelist Muriel Barbery has twelve-year-old Paloma, the central character, saying things

like "life is absurd" (p. 23), and "people still believe [foolishly] they're not here by chance" (p. 52), and "I was convinced very early on of the pointlessness of my existence" (p. 107). Spanish novelist Arturo Perez-Reverte has the protagonist in *The Painter of Battles* (trans. Margaret Sayers Peden [New York: Random House, 2009]) say that "life . . . [is] a perilous excursion toward death and nothingness" (p. 12). Carol Shields's Pulitzer Prize-winning *Unless* (Toronto: Random House, 2003) tells the story of a woman with a happy marriage and fulfilling work whose daughter nevertheless suddenly disappears, finally surfacing as a beggar on the streets of Toronto—a tale of loneliness and isolation between mother and daughter *in extremis*. The unidentified narrator of Diane Schoemperlen's *Our Lady of the Lost and Found* (Toronto: HarperCollins, 2001) finds her loneliness deeply intertwined with the fear that "my whole life is utterly devoid of meaning" (p. 324).

Chapter 4

What an Evangelical Common Worship Service Looks Like

We have established the principles of a distinctively evangelical common worship—principles derived from the theological emphases of evangelicalism. However, these principles *by themselves* do not provide the framework or structure of a worship service. Rather they are the emphases that will mark distinctively evangelical worship. The next step is to take these emphases and integrate them into an actual framework or structure of worship: the "order of service." To do that requires that we carefully set out the biblical pattern of common worship, into which the evangelical emphases will then fit. All the while, we have to keep in mind that the focus of common worship is God—and God alone—that "*worship is never meant to serve any other purpose except the glory of God.* The end of worship is worship."[1] Anything else amounts to a secularization of worship.

Why a Structure at All?

Many evangelicals will wonder why they should be concerned about the structure of common worship—the "order of service"—at all. Christopher Ellis, an English Baptist, is well aware of this when he writes, "So why bother with the sequence in which things happen in a service? Surely we should be more concerned with the sincerity of the worship leader and the congregation than with . . . a fixed running order. . . . What about being open to the guidance of the Holy Spirit?"[2] For many evangelicals, these concerns are deeply important. Realizing that God is sovereign and the Spirit moves as God wills, evangelicals are wary of common worship being turned into something rote. We do not imagine that we can somehow safely contain God by means of any order of service! And of course, since God is sovereign, we must always remain open to the divine leading in worship.

So why *should* we concern ourselves with the structure of worship at all? Let me suggest five reasons.

First, we need to be concerned about the structure because, according to the Bible, God is concerned about it. As evangelicals, one of our historic principles—what Bebbington called "biblicism"—is the conviction that Scripture is authoritative in all matters of faith and practice. As we have already seen from Scripture, God is *not* indifferent about *how* he is worshipped. This is, after all, the God who gave to the Israelites excruciatingly detailed instructions for his worship both in the wilderness tabernacle and in the temple in Jerusalem. We do not get to choose *how* we will worship God, and whenever people tried to worship God in *their* way in the Bible, it did not go well. Cain's offering to God was refused (Gen 3:5),[3] and shortly thereafter we are reading about the first murder. Korah and his compatriots were dramatically put to death by God when they decided *they* would worship God—offering incense—as *they*, rather than God, saw fit (Lev 10:1-3). What would be the sense of the psalm writer enjoining his readers to "Offer right sacrifices, and put your trust in the LORD" (Ps 4:5) if it were not possible to offer *wrong* sacrifices and *distrust* the Lord? Similarly, since Jesus said that his Father wanted as worshippers those who would worship in spirit and truth (John 4:23-24), it must be possible to worship in a way that is without the Spirit and is untruthful. Since God does care—a great deal—about divine worship, we must diligently search the Scriptures to discover how *God* wants to be worshipped. It is not up to us to decide. And structure apparently *is* one of the things about worship that matters to God. After all, God "is a God not of disorder" (1 Cor 14:33), and the apostle Paul instructs the disorderly Corinthians that everything in worship is to "be done decently and in order" (1 Cor 14:40). How we worship, including the order and structure of our common worship, matters enormously. As Baptist pastor and professor J. Daniel Day puts it,

> There is a definable 'thing' called the Christian worship of God with characteristics that constitute its unique integrity and therefore what purports to be the worship of God cannot be determined . . . by majority vote . . . it must incorporate enduring essentials or open itself to the charge of being something less than the worship of God.[4]

Second, common worship—worship to which God is not indifferent—is intended to be a journey. It's not an aimless, meandering journey. It's a clearly marked map that requires us to visit several quite specific places along the way to the final destination. The map isn't something we can safely ignore, because according to Scripture, God *intends* that we take this specific route for the benefit of our souls. With apologies to John Bunyan, we are to ascend the mountaintop of praise and adoration of God but then descend to the Valley of the Shadow of Death. In that dark and gloomy place, we face and admit our sins. This could become our "slough of despond" if we did not hear words assuring us of God's forgiveness, mercy, and love. The word of God sustains us for the ongoing journey, and we reach our destination, which sends us back out into the wider world to bear witness to God's love by word and deed.

The order of service matters, third, because what happens (or doesn't happen) and in what order things happen on Sunday morning *all* convey important messages. The order is *not* value neutral. It says something. The question is whether what is being said reflects the biblical worldview in which God is absolutely and always the centre, or a secular worldview in which God is secondary.

Fourth, a weekly pattern or structure reinforces in powerful ways the core story of our faith. For many evangelicals the worry is that "a pattern of worship repeated week after week soon becomes routinized and a recipe for boredom,"[5] a question that Thomas Long, professor of preaching at Emory University, answers by saying, "As a matter of fact . . . when it comes to human rituals, the more powerful they are the less they tend to change. . . . A congregation that can never change its pattern of worship is certainly in trouble, but a congregation that can change its worship every week is in much deeper trouble."[6] Surely in instructing Israel regularly to observe a pattern of festivals that were not to vary from year to year, God knew what he was doing. Why would Jesus have instructed his disciples to take a meal together repeatedly, a meal that was *each* time to include the same foods—bread and wine—if pattern was not important? We routinely observe everything from family birthdays (first the cake, then the presents, or vice-versa), Christmas (some families always open presents on Christmas Eve, others on Christmas Day), and national days according to specific rituals and structure, and indeed get quite annoyed or upset if the order is changed. Despite this experience, somehow we fail to realize that patterns are also important for our spiritual growth! We recognize that physiotherapy, athletic training, and learning to play a musical instrument all require repetition and pattern, but for some reason when it comes to our souls, we think that repetition and pattern are unnecessary!

Finally, a structure for common worship makes great freedom possible. That may sound paradoxical, but it shouldn't. We know from Scripture it is only in slavery to Christ that we find true freedom, the freedom to be what we were created to be—creatures living in right relationship with God, other humans, and the whole creation. Outside of that slavery to Christ is not freedom, but the misery of purposeless existence and endless doomed-to-failure attempts to find some point to life. Within the structure for common worship given in Scripture, we are enabled to join ourselves to the great never-ending worship of all creation. We do not endlessly have to keep trying one new thing after another in an effort to do so. We do not have to reinvent the wheel every Sunday, and there is profound relief in realizing that. Instead, our creativity can find expression *within* the structure that is given to us as a free gift from God, a gift of grace. To use a musical analogy,

> For some, an order of worship might feel like a straitjacket, limiting creativity. But consider jazz music. Jazz features spontaneous improvisation. But jazz improvisation works *only* because the musicians in a jazz combo are following a regular, predictable, repeated chord structure. Without this structure, the music would be chaos. Meaningful spontaneity happens *within* structure.[7]

The Fourfold Pattern for Common Worship

When the people of God gather then for Sunday worship, the "order of service" is not accidental or simply because "we've always done it that way." The structure of common worship should be determined by our very best understanding of who God is, what God is about, what God expects and wants, and who we are in relationship to God. Especially as evangelicals, for answers to those questions, we turn to Scripture. While different circumstances may sometimes mean changes are appropriate, certain elements of common worship will remain constant because God, according to Scripture, never changes: "I the LORD do not change," declared God through the prophet Malachi (Mal 3:6). Moreover, the various parts of a worship service logically occur in a particular order. When we ask questions about a worship service such as "Why are we doing this?" or "Why are doing this now, and not earlier or later?" we are in fact doing theology of worship. *We are asking whether our worship truly reflects what we have come to know about God from the Bible.*

Scripture provides a clear, basic, and simple pattern for common worship. This fourfold pattern is sometimes called the "catholic," the universal, pattern because it has been recognized, understood, and used by Christians since the earliest days of the church.[8] The four elements in order are Awe and Praise, Confession of Sin and Assurance of Pardon, God's Word, and Our Response.

While it is true that the New Testament does not give us a full description of a worship service, each of the elements in the fourfold pattern can be seen in the glimpses of the early church's worship that we are given. If Acts 2:42 is a summary description of worship right after the day of Pentecost, two of the four elements—Word ("the apostles' teaching") and Response ("the breaking of bread and the prayers") are present in order. Similarly, John's revelation gives us a glimpse of heaven's perfect worship in chapters 4 through 6. There we can distinguish awe and praise (in the singing by the living creatures of God's holiness, the twenty-four elders prostrating themselves and throwing their crowns before God's throne), confession of sin (no one is found worthy enough to open the scrolls), and the word (in the form of the same scrolls). One notes that the descriptions of worship in the patristic era—the three hundred years between the resurrection and the politicizing of the church under Constantine—clearly follow this same pattern. It would be imprudent indeed to ignore this reality—even though evangelicals do not consider the writings of the early fathers to have the same level of authority as Scripture—for these believers were much closer to the founding period and the apostolic age than we are.

Not surprisingly, however, given God's unchanging nature, this fourfold pattern goes back even before the birth of Jesus to the Old Testament. Likely the clearest example of this fourfold pattern is found in Isaiah 6:1-8. Here can be seen, in order, all four elements.

Encountering God Results in Awe and Praise

On entering God's presence, Isaiah (and we) are awestruck by God's majesty, power, love, and grace. The only appropriate response is praise.

> In the year that king Uzziah died I saw also the LORD sitting upon a throne, high and lifted up, and his train filled the temple. Above it stood the seraphims: each one had six wings; with twain he covered his face, and with twain he covered his feet, and with twain he did fly. And one cried unto another, and said, Holy, holy, holy, is the Lord of hosts: the whole earth is full of his glory. And the posts of the door moved at the

voice of him that cried, and the house was filled with smoke. (Isa 6:1-4, AV)

Confession of Sin and Assurance of Pardon

However, as soon as we encounter God, we realize our own sinfulness and our need to ask for forgiveness. Hence Isaiah cries out, "Woe is me! for I am undone; because I am a man of unclean lips, and I dwell in the midst of a people of unclean lips: for mine eyes have seen the King, the LORD of hosts" (Isa 6:5, AV). In accordance with God's repeated promises, genuine confession and sincere repentance leads to pardon. Thus, Isaiah's confession of sin leads to words of pardon: "Then flew one of the seraphims unto me, having a live coal in his hand, which he had taken with the tongs from off the altar: And he laid it upon my mouth and said, Lo, this hath touched thy lips and thine iniquity is taken away and thy sin purged" (Isa 6:6-7, AV).

The Word of God

Having confessed our sins, we are now ready—and able—to hear God's word to us. So also Isaiah, after confession and pardon, hears God's word to him: "I heard the voice of the Lord saying, Whom shall I send, and who will go for us?" (Isa 6:8a, AV)

Of course in the church's common worship we primarily hear God's word to us not by means of dramatic visions but through the Scriptures that are first read and then proclaimed/taught by means of the sermon. The point however is the same: God has something to say to his people.

Our Response to God

Once God's word is heard, we need to respond, to take action. That's exactly what Isaiah does. Once he hears God's word, he does not hesitate. He responds at once, saying, "Here am I; send me" (Isa 6:8b). This is where the "activism" that Bebbington described as so prominent among evangelical Christians enters the picture. The word leads to action in the wider world. We go out from common worship to change the world for Christ.

Examining the Fourfold Pattern in Detail

Since Scripture gives us this fourfold pattern for common worship, it's important to examine each element in detail. In particular, we need to see how the four elements work out, practically, for Sunday morning worship *and* see how the distinct evangelical emphases fit into the fourfold pattern.

Before we do that, however, it is essential to point out that this fourfold pattern *does not* imply or require a "formal" worship style in a cathedral-like setting, with preaching robes, choir anthems, or only "standard" hymns. It is quite possible, indeed desirable, for worship to be culturally sensitive and to use a variety of kinds of music that may or may not aesthetically agree with the tastes of particular individuals. What may be quite appropriate in a storefront mission in the ghetto of an American city would be culturally inappropriate in a university chapel; what fits well with a small rural church would clash violently with the cultural milieu of a suburban congregation in Toronto or a centre city church in Manhattan. Our model is the incarnation itself. Just as God in Jesus became fully human but without sin, so common worship should be culturally sensitive without being co-opted by a secular worldview. The crucial thing is to ensure that regardless of setting, musical style, or anything else, the worship has theological integrity—and that means it needs clearly to follow the fourfold pattern.

This pattern permits a great deal of flexibility and variation. *Within the fourfold pattern, there is a great deal of freedom.* Evangelicals generally understand from Scripture that it is in slavery to Christ that we find not our being restricted, cabined, cribbed, confined, or limited but rather real freedom. Over and over again Scripture teaches that real freedom is not the freedom to do whatever we please but the freedom to be and become what we were created to be. When Adam and Eve listened to the evil one and decided to eat the forbidden fruit, they fell for the oldest lie. Instead of being more free—like God—they found themselves less free, banished from the garden. Or to use a contemporary example, the astronaut on a space walk is tethered to the international space station by a cord that provides heat and oxygen. Suppose she decides she wants to be "free" and cuts that cord. Is she then free? Well, yes—"free" to die in the freezing cold, deprived of what is essential for life (oxygen). It's a tragically false freedom. If we understand the apparent paradox from Scripture that slavery to God is the only way to have true freedom, why do we have difficulty with the idea that within the bounds of a biblical structure of worship we find not restriction but freedom? R. Kent Hughes is the senior minister emeritus of College Church in Wheaton, Illinois, a church with strong historic ties to Wheaton College. His observations, though referring specifically to the free church tradition in the United States, are far more widely applicable:

> For more than 150 years the Free Church tradition operated on the "Scripture only" principle. The last two centuries brought change. In

America, where the Free Church tradition had once meant the freedom to order corporate worship according to the Scriptures, it came to mean the freedom to order such worship as one pleased.... Free Church Biblicism deteriorated into Free Church pragmatism.[9]

We are not free, in any aspect of our lives, to do as we please. We are slaves to Christ, but paradoxically, in that slavery we find real freedom. Outside of slavery to Christ is cold death, not freedom. The same applies to common worship. With this in mind, let's proceed to look at each of the four elements of common worship with an eye both to practical details and to how the distinctive evangelical emphases fit into the fourfold pattern.

Encountering God Results in Awe and Praise

This, the first of the four elements in worship, can have the following parts: the Gathering of God's People, Introit, Greeting, Call to Worship, Prayer of Invocation/The Collect, Hymn, Song or Chorus of Praise, and Affirmation of Faith.

The Gathering of God's People. It is not just Isaiah whose encounter with God left him awestruck. Scripture is filled with stories of individuals or groups encountering God, and almost inevitably such an encounter is pictured as resulting in awe, even fear. When God appears to the aged Abraham, he falls on his face, that is, he prostrates himself (Gen 17:1-3). When God speaks to Moses from the burning bush, the fearful Moses "hid his face for he was afraid to look upon God" (Exod 3:6). Later, at Mount Sinai, the people of Israel are warned to prepare carefully for an encounter with God (Exod 19:10-15). Even so, the people ask Moses to speak to them on God's behalf, fearing that hearing God directly will kill them (Exod 20:19). Later when Moses asks to see God's glory, God answers that to see God's face—fully to experience God's presence—would mean death (Exod 33:20). People in ancient Israel are frequently depicted as prostrating themselves when they experience a close encounter with God (for examples, Exod 12:27; Lev 9:24; Num 20:6; Judg 13:19-21; 1 Kings 18:39; 1 Chr 21:16; 2 Chr 7:3; Ezek 1:28; 3:23; 43:1-3). Peter, after the miraculous catch of fish early in Jesus' public ministry, falls down before Jesus saying, "Depart from me; for I am a sinful man, O Lord" (Luke 5:8, AV).

Doesn't all of this suggest that if we are serious about seeking God's presence in worship, we ought to do so in a reverent, utterly attentive, and respectful way? But is that what actually happens when evangelicals gather for Sunday worship? "All too often," wrote Robert Webber, "the atmosphere seems to work against reverence. Our churches are characterized by a feeling of over familiarity.... in the approach to God. The sense of transcendence and the otherness and holiness of God seems to be missing."[10] In many evangelical churches, the ten or fifteen minutes before the worship service begins—the gathering—are marked by loud conversation, instrument tuning, sound checks, and upbeat music. None of this is conducive to preparing to encounter God—insomuch as anyone can be prepared for such a thing! The American writer Annie Dillard suggests that perhaps we just don't realize what we're doing, or, worse, perhaps we don't really believe what we claim we do:

> On the whole, I do not find Christians ... sufficiently sensible of conditions. Does anyone have the foggiest idea what sort of power we so blithely invoke? Or ... does no one believe a word of it? ... we should all be wearing crash helmets. Ushers should issue life preservers and signal flares; they should lash us to our pews. For the sleeping god may wake someday and take offense or the waking god may draw us out to where we can never return.
>
> The eighteenth-century Hasidic Jews had more sense, and more belief. One Hasidic slaughterer, whose work required invoking the Lord, bade a tearful farewell to his wife and children every morning before he set out for the slaughterhouse. He felt, every morning, that he would never see any of them again. For every day, as he himself stood with his knife in his hand, the words of his prayer carried him into danger. After he called on God, God might notice and destroy him before he had time to utter the rest, "Have mercy."[11]

Evangelicals, who take with utmost seriousness the description of God given in Scripture as the Almighty Creator of all things, should approach common worship as a dangerous activity. "The mood [should be] ... one of quiet humility and openness before God.... It is appropriate to be pensive, meditative, and low-key."[12] This is *not* in any way to suggest that the atmosphere should be dour and grim. Reverent, respectful, quiet, and expectant does not preclude joy or anticipation of what is to come! Nor is any of this to suggest that there is no place for fellowship in the life of the church. Of course there is—just *not* as a part of common worship.

How, practically, can this be encouraged, modeled, and taught? Pastors might begin by checking their own behaviour. For most clergy, the ten or fifteen minutes before Sunday morning worship begins is busy, attending to last-minute details—everything from the Scripture reader or soloist who fails to show at the last moment to a sound system that is being suddenly uncooperative. Often it seems this is the time when congregants think it's a good idea to sidle up to the pastor for a conversation. All of these things do need attention. But the way one goes about attending to them is important. Does the congregation see their minister rushing frantically about, or does she or he move deliberately and quietly? Important pastoral care may well be provided in those pre-service conversations. One way to deal with this and also to encourage preparation is to make oneself available and visible for these kinds of conversations up until about ten to fifteen minutes before the service begins, but thereafter to absent oneself from the sanctuary or entryway of the church. Musicians, soloists, and choirs may need to be asked to finish any tuning or practice by a specified time, say, a quarter hour before the service is scheduled to begin. Those responsible for music in these moments, particularly "praise and worship" teams, may need to be given gentle guidance so that their music encourages people to reflect and prepare. Ideally, pastors and musicians will work closely together, with an understanding of what the goal is. Congregations unused to this time of quiet preparation for worship should not have the practice foisted upon them without explanation or warning. That approach is almost certain to create a backlash. Taking time to introduce the practice *and* giving a careful explanation of why the change is being made are critical. One might begin with one or two sermons, exegeting some of the texts of Scripture that depict the awestruck response of people who encounter God and pointing out the practical implications of this for Sunday worship. Perhaps at ten minutes before the service begins, an announcement may be made from the pulpit on these lines: "We will shortly begin our service of worship. Now is the time to prepare to encounter our God. Please begin to still yourselves. Pray that we may truly worship God. Read the Scripture lessons for this morning. Let us be quiet together and listen for God." A similar notice, which could include a suggested prayer, could appear in the service bulletin.

Introit. Those giving leadership in common worship also need to prepare. In many, perhaps most evangelical churches, it is customary for these folk to gather for prayer before the worship service begins. This usually happens in a room or office apart from the sanctuary. Their entry to the sanctuary is often a signal that the service of worship is beginning. The practical question then is, how and when do these people enter the sanctuary? There are many possibilities, some better than others. Having clergy, choir, or other worship leaders enter in piecemeal fashion whenever they choose does not convey a message of order but of chaos—not something we ascribe to God. If possible, all should enter together. The traditional way of achieving this was for a short piece of music, called the introit, to be sung as those giving leadership entered. Often this was a psalm set to music, but it might equally well be a contemporary chorus focusing on the praise and adoration of God.

Greeting. In many evangelical churches the first words actually spoken during a worship service have little to do with God. "Good morning! How are you?" or something similar followed by an injunction encouraging those present to introduce themselves to those sitting nearby is no different from what we experience in day-to-day life, in a business meeting, at the Rotary Club, or in a seminar. But this *is* different. This is God's people gathered for worship, focused on God, so how is God somehow left out of the greeting?

A greeting that keeps worshippers focused on God is needed instead. There are many ways of accomplishing this. For centuries Christian worship began with the pastor saying something like, "Welcome in the name of the Father, the Son, and the Holy Spirit. The Lord be with you," to which the people responded "And also with you." (On Easter Sunday the greeting was altered to "Christ is risen" and the response became a joyful "He is risen indeed!") Thereafter, people may be invited to "greet one another in the Lord." Perhaps they may be encouraged actually to use the ancient formula, "The Lord be with you . . . and also with you" as they shake hands or instead to say, "The peace of Christ be with you . . . and also with you." The specific words are not so important as the fact that they continue to keep everyone focused on God.

Call to Worship. A Call to Worship is intended simply to remind everyone why they are there. It says, "This is why we are here, let us begin." It also serves to announce, "God is active and present. We need to pay attention." The call to worship also serves an intensely practical purpose as Robert Rayburn observes:

> Very few are actually ready to worship God when they arrive in the church sanctuary. Some have been in a Sunday School class where they have been bored by poor teaching or by a lesson which they did not feel was relevant to their needs. Some may have been upset by family friction which developed in their automobiles on the way to church. Some may be struggling with severe temptations known only to themselves. Others may have their minds occupied by important business decisions which

must be made during the coming week. . . . The call to worship must, just as far as possible, secure their attention for the all-important activity . . . of corporate communion with God.[13]

Very often the Call to Worship should be a text from Scripture, and this practice aligns well with the evangelical emphasis on Scripture—what Bebbington called "biblicism." All of common worship should be soaked in Scripture. The psalms are the primary source for calls to worship from Scripture. On rare occasions, one of the Scriptural laments may be employed as the call to worship. This would be appropriate, for example, if a local or national tragedy occurred in the preceding week and will be a focus for the day's sermon, or for a worship service marking the beginning of Lent.

Occasionally a Call to Worship may take the form of the minister speaking outside of Scripture, addressing briefly the importance of worship or what happens to us in worship. This approach should be used sparingly and with care. The danger is that it can easily turn into a rambling "introduction" involving what the minister is personally thinking or feeling at that moment.

One final important observation about the Call to Worship. We *do not* call *ourselves* to worship, neither does the officiant call the congregation to worship. Rather God, albeit through the voice of a fallen human being, calls us to worship. We are not in control even at the beginning of common worship—God is! John Jefferson Davis points out,

> In the call to worship we realize that the meeting is no merely human meeting, planned and controlled by human agenda, but a special meeting called by God, on his divine authority, for the purpose of meeting with his people. . . . We are called to lay aside our personal agenda, to realize where we are and what we are to be doing, to focus our attention on the unseen God, and to yield to him our full awareness and attention.[14]

Prayer of Invocation or The Collect. The first prayer of the service of worship may take the form of invocation, collect, or a combination of the two. In many evangelical churches it is simply called the opening prayer.

To invoke means "to call upon." In a prayer of invocation, we are calling upon God to be powerfully present by God's Spirit, to guide and direct the service of worship that it may be pleasing and honouring to God. The person leading a prayer of invocation should *always* be mindful of what a dangerous thing she or he is doing. It is no small or routine thing to call upon the Creator of all things. As Thomas Long puts it,

> "We seek your face, O God" we pray with hardly a thought of what we are saying, forgetting that the One whose presence we so casually invoke summons the creation out of nothing, commands the moon and the stars to sing, shatters kingdoms and brings tyrants to their knees, shakes the foundations of the world, and causes the earth to melt at a single word.[15]

A "collect" (pronounced "Call–ect") refers to the "collecting" of the prayers of those assembled in a short, summary form. This kind of prayer will often introduce the theme that those who have planned the worship service intend to weave throughout it. Since the person praying is praying on behalf of and with the congregation, prayers during common worship should never use the first person singular "I" but always "we."

Regardless of which kind of prayer is used, the leader should take care to avoid "precious" or flowery language and hackneyed expressions such as "Lord, we just want to . . . ." Confusing wording or bad grammar should also be avoided. Do these things really matter? The simple answer is yes. In one's private prayers, these things do not matter, *but* in public prayer the intention is that the people of God are praying *along with* the one who is speaking aloud. It's difficult to do that if the words being spoken are distracting. When worshippers finds themselves thinking, "What did *that* mean?" because of poor grammar or confusing wording, cringing inwardly because of trite language, or "tuning out" because of the use of the same expressions or phrases week after week, they are no longer fully engaged in praying *with* the person speaking.

Hymn, Song, or Chorus of Praise. Since the focus of the church's worship is to be on God and acknowledging his worth, then logically an act of praise to God, such as a hymn, worship chorus (or choruses), or psalm of praise follows the invocation.

Whatever music is sung should clearly be an adoring and praising of God, an acknowledging of God's supreme worth. This means that lyrics—words—matter. It is almost always extremely questionable to use hymns or choruses that are about what "I" or "we" are thinking, feeling, doing, or desiring. Such lyrics shift the attention away from God to the worshipper and amount to a secularization of worship. They are therefore especially inappropriate for use as an act of praise to God. The words of a hymn or chorus also matter in terms of what they actually say about God. Some contemporary choruses frankly say almost nothing about God. Others, while they say something valid and accurate, repeat the same words so many times that one gets the impression they are some kind of Christian "mantra." The God made known to us in Scripture, however, bids us love him with our minds. Unlike some of the great Eastern faiths and much of the new age movement, our goal is not to reach a state of mental oblivion or emptiness but to bring our minds into full alignment with God's ways and God's thinking. Always, music must be chosen not because it is upbeat or popular but on the basis of what meaning is conveyed by the lyrics.

Keep in mind that every worship service in general, and every hymn, song, or chorus of praise in particular, are and are meant to be deeply countercultural acts. They are assertions that what our society says is important and central is not so important and central. The people of God need to be constantly and *explicitly* reminded that they are engaged in a countercultural activity. "Every time we sing praise to the triune God, we are asserting our opposition to anything that would attempt to stand in God's place."[16]

Two final observations: churches where the custom is to have several choruses in a row should be cautious. First, the widespread custom of asking the congregation to stand for ten or fifteen minutes is difficult for and insensitive to the elderly and to those with mobility problems. Consider other options. Second, those in leadership roles should avoid using phrases that imply that this period of extended singing is the sum total of worship. Saying things like "Let's worship God" or "Let's worship God again" in reference to this time of singing strongly implies that nothing else we are doing is part of worship! It's unlikely that is what those who use these expressions mean, but once again, words matter!

Affirmation of Faith. An affirmation of faith may be placed here if the intention is to continue the act of praise or to affirm who we are as the gathered people of God. Alternatively, such an affirmation may be understood as "response," in which case it would come closer to the end of the worship service.

An affirmation can take many different forms. One of the great historic creeds of the church—the Apostles' or Nicene—might be read together. Another possibility is to read together a statement of faith that especially relates to the theme of the Scripture readings and sermon. For example, in a worship service that focuses on God's intention that there be peace and justice in his world, the following affirmation—in this case drawn from the Iona Community in Scotland—might be used:

We believe in God
Whose love is the source of all life
And the desire of our lives,
Whose love was given a human face
In Jesus of Nazareth,
Whose love was crucified by the evil
That waits to enslave us all
And whose love, defeating even death,
Is our glorious promise of freedom.
Therefore, though we are sometimes fearful
And full of doubt,
In God we trust;
And, in the name of Jesus Christ,
We commit ourselves, in the service of others,
To seek justice and to live in peace,
To care for the earth
And to share the commonwealth
Of God's goodness,
To live in the freedom of forgiveness
And the Power of the Spirit of Love,
And in the Company of the Faithful
So to be the Church,
For the Glory of God. Amen.[17]

As we become increasingly conscious of the worldwide nature of the church, we may also draw upon the insights of Christians from other parts of the world. Their words in statements of faith can reveal for us new things from Scripture, or old things that we have forgotten or overlooked. Here, for example is the "Korean Creed":

We believe in the one God, maker and ruler of all things, Father of all men [sic], the source of all goodness and beauty, all truth and love.

We believe in Jesus Christ, God manifest in the flesh, our teacher, example, and Redeemer, the Savior of the world.

We believe in the Holy Spirit, God present with us for guidance, for comfort, and for strength.

We believe in the forgiveness of sins, in the life of love and prayer, and in grace equal to every need.

We believe in the Word of God contained in the Old and New Testaments as the sufficient rule both of faith and of practice.

We believe in the Church as the fellowship for worship and for service of all who are united to the living Lord.

We believe in the kingdom of God as the divine rule in human society, and in the brotherhood [sic] of man [sic] under the fatherhood of God.

We believe in the final triumph of righteousness, and in the life everlasting.[18]

Other examples include the "Masai Creed," produced by the Masai people of Eastern Africa, working together with partner missionaries,[19] an "anti-poverty Creed" from Kairos Southern Africa, written by Reverend Edwin Arrison (which reminds us of God's special concern for the poor),[20] and the Church of North India's Mission Statement (which includes reference to breaking down the caste system in that country).[21]

Individuals or groups within the church might be asked to compose a statement of faith on a particular theme. Individual congregations and denominations often have their own statements of faith. Many churches, particularly in the Baptist, Congregationalist, and Methodist traditions have "church covenants" that are foundational to their identity. These too can be used as affirmations of faith.

Confession of Sin and Assurance of Pardon

In one form or another each of the four original branches—Anabaptist, Anglican, Lutheran and Reformed—of the Reformation included confession in their worship services. Even the phrasing of the prayers of confession in the Anglican Book of Common Prayer for morning and evening prayer and the celebration of Eucharist have been widely adopted by many denominations in the English-speaking world. Luther's German Mass of 1526 included confession.[22] Among the Reformed, Zwingli's 1525 Liturgy of the Word,[23] Martin Bucer's Strassburg liturgy of 1536,[24] Calvin's "Form of Church Prayers"[25] for Geneva, and John Knox's "Forme of Prayers" of 1556[26] all gave prominent place to confession of sin. Balthasar Hubmaier, the earliest of the Anabaptist theologians, not only included confession as part of common worship but also came close to turning it into a third sacrament![27] Historically, evangelicals were not shy about saying that the chief human problem was sin. One need only read some of the sermons of Whitefield, Wesley, or Edwards to discover this! This is hardly surprising given that they were merely reflecting Scripture. Quite simply put, "Without faith, it is impossible to please God, but without repentance it is impossible to get started in the life of faith."[28]

But in a secular society, saying that we are sinners is considered extremely distasteful, offensive, and perhaps even slightly psychotic. If anything, we think it is not us but God who has some answering to do! We *may* admit we have "made mistakes" or "had failures" or that we "failed to maximize our potential," but that is about as far as it goes. Even then we are quick to point to mitigating circumstances to justify ourselves—"I had a difficult childhood," "I was under a lot of pressure," "everyone is doing it," "everyone is not only doing it but also doing far worse than I've done," "I'd had a lot to drink," "the rules are stupid anyway."

What is truly alarming is that this attitude seems to be mirrored in many evangelical worship services. We have abandoned both the wisdom and practice of the Protestant Reformers *and* the early evangelicals. Weekly confession of sin during common worship is seen as depressing, and so it has disappeared entirely from many evangelical worship services. Why? Perhaps because both praise *and* confession run contrary to what our secular culture tells us and we are seriously co-opted by that culture? In praise, the importance of humanity in general—and the individual worshipper in particular—is reduced, while God's importance is exalted. That is bad enough! But confession is even worse! In confession, we are making ourselves vulnerable, acknowledging our need, declaring we are not independent but dependent; we are admitting we need to do things in God's way—and we haven't.

Yet at least three of the by-products of worship focused on God hinge very much on confession of sin. We will not find *meaning* if our lives fail to acknowledge the reality of our estrangement from God, others, and the wider creation. Neither will we be *formed* increasingly to resemble Jesus if we ignore the reality that there are parts of our lives that are not fully obedient to God. Confession of sin is essential for solid spiritual formation. And of course, we are hardly going to learn to be countercultural people who think, live, and act in Kingdom ways as opposed to the ways of a secular culture if we buy into our culture's notion that sin isn't really real. William Dyrness of Fuller Theological Seminary reminds us,

> confession in the worship service is a means by which we constantly get reoriented to the way things [really] are. This reorienting is not to the way we think or feel things are, but to the way they actually are. While the world around us may try to convince us that we are really OK, in

confession we acknowledge that we constantly go astray, that even our good works are marked by sin, and that apart from God's grace we are lost.[29]

Normally the logical place for confession is immediately after the various acts of praise, for in entering into God's presence, just like Isaiah, we become powerfully aware of our sinfulness. Occasionally, however, a variation makes sense. For instance, a worship service with a penitential theme, such as Good Friday, might conclude with a time for confession.

Call to confession. A call to confession is simply an invitation to come before God to acknowledge our sins. In some churches, the call to confession may include a reading of the Ten Commandments or the Great Commandment of Jesus. Often it includes a brief explanation of *why* we need to do this—because we have, as individuals, done things our way instead of God's way, sin is our biggest problem as human beings that estranges us from God, and we need to seek God's forgiveness in order to find reconciliation. Confession is also an acknowledgment that we are part of a sinful society and we bear corporate as well as individual guilt.

But there is another reason for confession, and that is simply that we cannot expect truly to "hear" the word without confession. Robert Benson in his book *Living Prayer* relates how in the midst of personal crisis, when Scripture seemed not to speak to him, he was given a piece of wise advice by a man he names only as Angus: "You cannot hear the Word right now . . . because there is no room in you for the Word right now. You must live in confession for a while, until you are empty enough to receive the Word."[30] In other words, in order to be filled by God through the Scriptures, we need to empty out that which is against God so there is room for God.

Prayer of confession. Prayers of confession can take an enormous variety of forms. A single person may lead the prayer—which can be the minister or a layperson. The prayer of confession might just as well involve several people. The prayer might include set responses (such us "Lord, have mercy") from the congregation, or a time for silent confession. It might, in certain circumstances, even include an opportunity for individuals publically to seek forgiveness of others in the congregation. Certainly the prayer of confession is also a teaching opportunity. Since much evangelicalism is individualistically focused and fails to see that in Scripture sin can be both individual *and* corporate, the prayer of confession can be an opportunity to acknowledge not just sins of individuals but also sins of entire groups—churches, communities, and whole nations. "Sin in all its multiple and insidious forms not only infects our individual lives but also disrupts community, deforms institutions, and even damages the creation itself."[31] Scripture clearly insists that there is such a thing as corporate responsibility, corporate sin, and corporate guilt. We need to acknowledge and confess that we are part of communities, nations, and economic, social, and political systems that are sinful and contrary to God's will for the world.

Whatever form the prayer of confession takes, there should be a conscious effort to connect it with the theme of the worship service, which of course is normally dictated by the Scriptures attended to on any particular Sunday. (Indeed, as a general rule, every element should tie into the theme of the service. This is simply good teaching methodology: "tell them what you're going to tell them, tell them, then tell them what you told them.")

Assurance of pardon. Having been countercultural, become vulnerable, and confessed our sins to God, it's now important to hear words assuring us of pardon or forgiveness. Some evangelicals may object that this smacks of the idea that the church or the minister has the power to forgive sin. Not so! Clearly, God alone can forgive sin. *But* the church, the minister, and indeed any Christian may confidently declare that God's promise that all who genuinely repent of sin and confess Christ as Lord are forgiven. Protestant Christians generally affirm belief in the priesthood of *all* believers, which means each of us is capable of acting in a priestly role for any other, and part of that role is to announce God's forgiveness.

The assurance of pardon is most likely to take the form of simply quoting or closely paraphrasing appropriate passages from the Bible. For instance, one could say, "Hear the good news. The central promise of Scripture is this: God did not send his Son, Jesus, into the world to condemn the world, but rather to set it free from sin. Everyone who believes in him has God's own promise of eternal life. Thanks be to God! Amen!"

The Word of God

The Word of God is the third element in the fourfold pattern for common worship that is described for us in Scripture.

For evangelicals, the word of God—that is the Bible—is of paramount importance. It is our guide to daily life and authoritative in matters of faith and practice. God, we believe, speaks to us through the word read (the Bible) and secondarily through the word preached (the sermon insofar as it is faithful to the Scriptures). Both the word read and the word preached point to the one who is *the* Word, and both are absolutely core to the evangelical tradition, what Bebbington described as "biblicism."

The word of God read. For evangelicals, the Bible is historically central to common worship. John Jefferson Davis sums up well why the reading of Scripture is so important:

> In the public reading of Scripture . . . we listen for God's voice speaking through the text that he himself has inspired and can now illuminate our understanding. We hear the divinely inspired words without human commentary before we hear the human commentary in the sermon. . . . We recognize that we, as humans, are not in control and not lords and masters of the Word of God.[32]

In recent decades, however, there has been a curious and troubling development in many evangelical churches—less and less Scripture is actually read aloud. It is not at all uncommon for there to be only two or three verses of Scripture read. For churches that proudly claim to be heirs of the Protestant Reformation, it is passing strange that far *less* Scripture is read on Sunday morning than in *any* Roman Catholic parish in the world and indeed in most of the so-called "mainline" Protestant churches.

There are multiple theological and practical problems with reading very little Scripture during common worship. First, this approach does not give Scripture anything more than a cursory part in Sunday morning worship. This simply does not align with historic evangelical theology's emphasis on the importance of Scripture. If the Bible truly is our guide to all of life, authoritative in matters of faith and practice, then we need to hear *much* more of it than just a couple of verses. Second, this approach almost never allows the congregation to hear anything even remotely like "*all* the counsel of God" (Acts 20:27, AV, emphasis added). For example, the Old Testament is almost never read.[33] Third, whether we like it or not, for many people in the pews, the *only* Scripture they hear or read in the course of a week is that which is read on Sunday morning. If even that is drastically reduced, why are we surprised by the degree of biblical illiteracy in our churches? Fourth, reading only two or three passages encourages proof texting rather than looking at passages in context, and fifth, it very often means that the Scripture passages read unconsciously tend to rotate among the pastor's (usually relatively few) favourite bits of the Bible. Worse still is when it's not just that only the pastor's favourite bits of Scripture are being read, but also when these verses are simply a peg on which to hang the preacher's thoughts. The sermon should normally be an exposition of the Bible reading, and it is important that preachers are subject to the reading, rather than manipulate the reading by making it fit what they want to say . . . a Bible reading of more than a couple of verses will enable the congregation to hear more easily the voice of Scripture and not just the voice of the preacher.[34]

And last, but by no means least, we need to keep in mind that the Bible is our source for knowing what is really real and important, as opposed to what the surrounding secular culture says is real and important. If we lose the Bible, we will inevitably be assimilated into the wider society in which we live.

What is to be done? Restoring the reading of Scripture to the prominent place it deserves may mean reducing the time given to some other elements of the worship service. For example, a former student once told me that in her church—which had very little Scripture reading—there "wouldn't be time" for any additional reading of the Bible. But the same congregation had time for fifteen or twenty minutes of praise choruses at the outset of morning worship! Surely if the choice is between cutting five or ten minutes of choruses so that much Scripture may be read or keeping fifteen to twenty minutes of choruses and reading little or none of the Bible, the decision, for evangelicals, should be obvious!

There are multiple resources for and approaches to reading Scripture during common worship. Some of these will be discussed in greater detail in the last chapter of this book. For now, however, I will mention two approaches. *Lectio Continua* (Latin for "continuous reading") was widely practiced among the Protestant Reformers. This is the practice of reading the Bible in sequence Sunday by Sunday. Every Sunday, the reading begins where the previous Sunday's reading finished. This approach strongly encourages expository preaching, as week by week, month after month, a pastor works his or her way through one book of Scripture after another. The approach that I personally favour is *Lectio Selecta* (Latin for "selected reading"), which means the use of a lectionary. A lectionary is simply a listing of Scripture passages appointed to be read on certain days, usually Sunday by Sunday. In this pattern, by long-standing custom, there are usually four readings (or "lessons") appointed for each Sunday—an Old Testament lesson, a Psalm, a reading from one of the Letters of the New Testament (usually called "The Epistle"), and last, in the place of honour, a reading from one of the four Gospels. Over the course of the centuries there have many, many lectionaries, but the Revised Common Lectionary is the most widely known and most widely used contemporary lectionary. It works on a three-year cycle that, if followed means that most of the "major" sections and stories of Scripture are read at least once.[35]

One final note pertaining to the reading of Scripture during common worship. Not everyone has the ability or the gift to read aloud well. Some people have soft voices, drop their voices at the end of sentences, or know nothing about projecting their voices, so they can be barely heard. Others, because of nervousness, poor eyesight, dyslexia, or simply poor reading skills, add or miss words, stumble and halt, or alternatively read so quickly that few listeners can keep up. Some read in a monotone. If Scripture is as important as we evangelicals say it is, then when it is read during common worship, it deserves to be read well and in such a way that everyone can hear it clearly. Therefore, whoever is reading Scripture should be chosen based on their ability to read it well.[36]

The word of God proclaimed (the sermon). For evangelicals, preaching, second only to the reading of the Scriptures, holds pride of place. We believe that, by God's Spirit, whenever preaching is faithful to Scripture, it becomes the very word of God *for us*, addressing us directly.

Once again, it is crucial to understand the meaning of words. What does preaching (the word proclaimed) mean? What is it supposed to do? What is its purpose? Preaching certainly *does not* mean any kind of speaking on a Sunday morning, not even talking about "religious" subjects.

One helpful definition of the purpose of preaching is "to help congregations make connections between Christian Scripture and their daily living as Christians."[37] Preaching is about equipping and teaching the followers of Jesus to live out their faith beyond Sunday morning worship and the interior of the church building. The preacher's job in the sermon is to help his or her people make every part of life sacred, subject to Christ's lordship, as opposed to secularism that restricts God to certain limited areas of life. Preaching that is faithful to the biblical pattern aims to turn every congregant into both a little theologian who knows how to think theologically with a specifically Christian worldview, and an activist who is engaged in the work of the Kingdom in daily life.

Another useful explanation of church in general (and the purpose of preaching in particular) is given by Tim Suttle in his book *Shrink: Faithful Ministry in a Church-Growth Culture*.

The task of ministry involves de-scripting ourselves and others from a story we are told by our society—a story that cannot make us safe or happy—and rescripting ourselves in the story we call the gospel. . . . *We are trying to switch stories.* We are working to change our stories from the old, tired script of individualism, consumerism, and nationalism, a failed script and a lie. And the health of our world depends on our ability to leave that old story and join God's new story. The only way to do this is through a *steady, patient, intentional articulation of a better story*, the story we call the gospel.[38]

Preaching is about "changing stories" from that of the surrounding secular culture to the story given to us in Scripture. Preaching means teaching, nudging, and encouraging the people of God to embrace, understand, and live out the new and better story of the gospel.

Regardless of which definition of the purpose of preaching you prefer, "The ultimate test" is, as Marva Dawn writes,

> whether sermons turn the hearers into theologians and activists. Do [sermons] grapple with texts and teach the people how to question? Do they wrestle with faith and invite the listeners to know that victory is assured? Do they struggle against the world's pain and challenge believers to create justice? *Above all, do they bring us all into God's presence to hear his Word to us?*[39]

Historically, Protestantism strongly emphasized both expository and doctrinal preaching. Expository preaching means carefully setting out the precise meaning of texts in their original context (exegesis) and then explaining how the text applies to life today (hermeneutics). Both parts of expository preaching—exegesis and hermeneutics—follow careful, systematic procedures.[40] For evangelicals, expository preaching was simply the logical outcome of Bebbington's "biblicism," a high view of the authority of the Bible. Convinced that Scripture was "more to be desired . . . than gold" (Ps 19:10, AV) and that it was the only safe "lamp unto my feet, and . . . light unto my path" (Ps 119:105, AV), evangelicals expected expository sermons that opened their eyes to "behold wondrous things" (Ps 119:18, AV). Indeed, the evangelical movement became renowned for producing generation upon generation of notable expository preachers, from Whitefield and Wesley to Spurgeon and Lloyd-Jones. Doctrinal preaching was also historically important for evangelicals. Doctrinal preaching (which requires no less attention to exegesis and hermeneutics than expository preaching) focuses on setting forth the great doctrines drawn from the Bible—for example the person and work of Christ, the incarnation, the Trinity—and explaining the importance, relevance, and application of these doctrines for present-day life. Robert Smith, Jr. says,

> the task of the doctrinal preacher is to serve as an escort who ushers the hearer into the presence of God through the proper and precise expounding of the Word of God. When this is done, the efforts of doctrinal preachers have reached their limits because they cannot transform the hearer. The hearer is left in the presence of the only One who can transform a human soul—Christ.[41]

By contrast, many evangelical pulpits today provide a steady diet of sermons that focus on "How to" fix this or that problem in life, improve one's finances, overcome illness, or have a more harmonious family life. Such preaching begins with a particular problem and then goes to Scripture to find a solution. While Scripture may still be present in such sermons, it is often not central. Instead of allowing the movement, at least most of the time, to be from Scripture to life, the movement is from life to Scripture. This kind of sermon may indeed sometimes be needful, but it should be used infrequently. The risk is having *my* problems and *my* concerns dictate the agenda, rather than God's word. We risk hearing only those parts of Scripture that provide an immediate answer to our current problems, rather than the whole counsel of God. Moreover, this kind of preaching tends to support the secularization of worship as it implies that Christianity is about adding or fitting a few "God things" into our lives as opposed to God's sovereign call on our lives and our making God the core and Lord of our lives. As Michael Horton puts it,

> the purpose of preaching is . . . not to find helpful tips for using God to make our lives a little less miserable. God does not get incorporated into our [story] but we into his. This narrative [of Scripture] is not there to give us some additional help in constructing our own life movie but to judge it and us with it, so we can finally give up on it and become a character in the [story] of redemption.
>
> . . . [God] comes not to offer banal support to our sagging self-confidence or to fix the unpleasantness of our daily existence . . . he doesn't come to fit in with our already established patterns of thought and life. He comes to dash our silly hopes and to expose our felt needs as

trivial, in order to give us new ones that are far greater, and then to satisfy those beyond our wildest dreams.[42]

In general, we come to common worship from a week in which a secular society has tried to shape our identity as something radically different than what Scripture says it is. Having moved God to the edges of life, a secular society values people not on the basis of their having been created by and loved by God—which makes each of us of enormous value. Instead, our culture usually measures value in terms of what we can do or accomplish. Why is it that the first question usually asked in a social situation is "What do you do?" Consider how our society treats those who are unable to produce or accomplish much—the unborn, children, elderly, sick, unemployed, underemployed, addicted, and mentally ill. Preaching that moves from "my problem(s)" to "solutions" often tends to support the secular way of looking at value and means we tend to think of our identity not in terms of our relationship with God but in terms of what we can produce. The problem is that

> when we seek a different identity derived from anything other than God, we don't actually become different but only return to the nothingness we were before God created our lives. This is what gathers in the pews of church every Sunday—creatures who believed the serpent's lie that their identity could be changed by reaching for something other than what they were given by the Creator. Some believed they could get a different, preferred identity if they only got married. Others thought they just needed to find a better job or buy a better home in order to have a better life. . . . And all that the reach for a different source to their identity has left them with is souls filled with primordial nothingness.[43]

Preaching that offers more of the same stuff, the same approach as our society, or that merely adds some kind of thin Christian veneer to the self-absorbed approach to life of the surrounding culture has been deeply secularized. "What the congregation needs is not a strategist to help them form [yet] another plan for achieving a desired image of life, but a poet who looks beneath even the desperation to recover the mystery of what it means to be made in God's image."[44] Our real identity as human beings, according to the Bible, is our identity as creatures, as children of the God made known to us best in Jesus Christ, and that is not only sufficient but also the *only* place we will find our true identity.

For centuries, members of the powerful Habsburg family that ruled the Austrian Empire (later Austria-Hungary) have been entombed in the Capuchin Church in Vienna. The most recent such entombment took place in 2011 for Otto von Habsburg, eldest son of the last emperor who actually reigned before the dissolution of the empire at the end of the First World War. In accordance with ancient custom, when the coffin carrying Otto von Habsburg's body arrived at the gates of the church, accompanied by the mourners, a herald knocked at the door. Inside, a Capuchin monk responded by asking, "Who demands entry?" The herald answered by listing all the royal and noble titles of the deceased:

> Otto of Austria; former Crown Prince of Austria-Hungary; Prince Royal of Hungary and Bohemia, of Dalmatia, Croatia, Slavonia, Galicia, Lodomeria, and Illyria; Grand Duke of Tuscany and Cracow; Duke of Lorraine, of Salzburg, Styria, Carinthia, Carniola and Bukowina; Grand Prince of Siebenbürgen, Margrave of Moravia; Duke of Silesia, Modena, Parma, Piacenza, Guastalla, Oświęcim and Zator, Teschen, Friaul, Dubrovnik and Zadar; Princely Count of Habsburg and Tyrol, of Kyburg, Gorizia and Gradisca; Prince of Trento and Brixen; Margrave of Upper and Lower Lusatia and Istria; Count of Hohenems, Feldkirch, Bregenz, Sonnenburg, etc.; Lord of Trieste, Kotor and Windic March, Grand Voivod of the Voivodeship of Serbia etc., etc.

The Capuchin monk responded, "We do not know him." The herald knocked a second time. Again the monk asked, "Who demands entry?" and this time the herald responded by listing Otto's numerous and impressive accomplishments, which included an earned PhD, authorship of dozens of books, and helping thousands of Jews to escape the Nazis during the Second World War. Habsburg had opposed the Nazi annexation of Austria, for which he was sentenced to death and had his personal and family property confiscated by the Nazis. He served as a member of the European Parliament, championed the cause of refugees and the sanctity of human life. But the Capuchin friar again responded, "We do not know him." Finally the herald knocked a third time, and once more the monk asked, "Who demands entry?" This time the herald responded simply, "Otto, a sinful human being." The monk inside at last replied, "Thus he may enter," and the doors were finally opened.[45] Just as for Otto von Habsburg, our real identity has nothing to do—as our secular society insists—with our societal position or achievements. Our real identity is found in our having been created by and loved by God. Period. Full stop.

Special care is needed with sermons preached on Sundays falling on or close to national holidays. It is frighteningly easy for such worship services and their sermons to become outstanding examples of Constantinian Christianity. Many evangelicals seem to have inordinate difficulty with the psalm writer's injunction to "Praise the LORD, O my soul" (Ps 146:1, AV) as opposed to putting our "trust in princes . . . in whom there is no help" (Ps 146:3, AV). Morning worship can become an hour or two spent praising not God but one's country, its values and distinctives, heroic historical figures, or supposed (but frequently historically and theologically untrue) "Christian" origins, values, and foundation or the supposed (again often historically and theologically untrue) Christian faith of national figures.[46] How is all this to be avoided? Short of ignoring the national observance entirely—an approach some clergy have in fact taken—references in the sermon to a national holiday should be relatively minor. Both the sermon and the entire worship service should make it patently clear that God and country are *not* identical, that for the follower of Jesus Christ, it can *never* be "my country, right or wrong."

Two final comments about the sermon in an evangelical service of common worship: "Wandering" preachers who wander up and down the aisles of the sanctuary instead of remaining behind the pulpit from which Scripture is read might wish to reconsider this approach. Does such wandering give the impression that the sermon is not tied to and strictly controlled by the Scripture? On a similar note, the reduction of the pulpit in many evangelical churches to a small Plexiglas lectern, or in some cases the elimination of the pulpit entirely, fails to communicate physically that the sermon is based solidly on Scripture. While older-style pulpits were perhaps overly ornate and large, the fact that they physically dwarfed the minister communicated the message that the minister was engulfed by Scripture and that any authority she or he held came solely from faithfully and carefully explaining Scripture. One of the things the incarnation means is that the physical—be that where and how much the preacher moves during the sermon or the size (or even existence) of the pulpit—matters. The physical not only matters but also usually "says" something important. We who believe in the incarnation should hardly be surprised by this. After all, we affirm that God's becoming a physical human being in Jesus mattered enormously and definitely said something of critical importance!

Response

The last of the four elements in common worship is response. Having heard God's word, Isaiah cried out, "Here am I! Send me!" (Isa 6:8, AV). Unfortunately in many evangelical worship services the opportunity for response by the people of God is severely limited. Here is one example. A worship service that ends with an "altar call" inviting non-Christians to come forward as a means of announcing their new commitment to Christ provides an opportunity for response only to non-Christians. In a secular society, what that means on most Sundays is that an opportunity for response is being given to people who aren't there but whom we wish were there! The response part of the common worship service should instead provide means for the people who are actually present, who for the most part are *already* followers of Jesus, to respond, preferably in several different ways, to the hearing of God's word.

It is critical that the movement toward response should *always* emphasize that the overwhelming majority of our response will happen after we have left the church building, in the hours and days that come *after* the benediction. If the worship has been as it ought to be, it is carried out into the week, and the concluding element of common worship should make this absolutely clear each and every Sunday. Edward H. Hammett puts it bluntly:

> The believers who meet as the gathered church for worship, praise, and equipping on Sundays fulfill their mission as the scattered church when they intentionally live out their faith in Christ throughout the week in the world. The scattered church is where 90 percent of the church's work can be accomplished. It is where the hurting are helped, the aimless are counseled, the bereaved are comforted, the imprisoned are visited, the naked are clothed, the lost are witnessed to, and the hungry are fed.[47]

"We are," Hammett writes, "called to disperse as God's people on mission during the week. . . . We are saved to penetrate the world for Christ. . . . [This is] a 'mission post' from which the gathered church scatters."[48]

The response element of the fourfold pattern may include the following parts: hymn, song, or chorus of response; notices; prayers of the people; offering; commissioning and benediction. Let's examine each of these in turn.[49]

Hymn, song, or chorus of response. From the outset, music has been an important part of Christian worship.[50] Music can sometimes touch the soul in ways that the spoken word cannot. The piece of music (in whatever style) that is chosen for the hymn, song, or chorus of response should actually be an opportunity for response. Most often this means a hymn or chorus with lyrics reminding, exhorting, or encouraging the people of God to go out into the wider world to bear witness to Christ by their words (evangelism) and actions, to promote peace and justice, and in general to work toward seeing the Kingdom of God (God's will) accomplished. Sometimes, depending on the Scripture texts, sermon, and major theme of the service, the appropriate response is a hymn of joyful praise and adoration. Occasionally, though rarely, a hymn or chorus of lament, or even confession/repentance, may be appropriate. (In this latter case, as suggested above, the Prayer of Confession might even be moved to the *end* of the worship service as a form of response.)

Notices. In many evangelical churches, the notices or announcements appear, incongruously, at some point five or ten minutes into the service. What this appears to say is that we're not quite sure what to do with the announcements, so let's get them over with as quickly as possible. That is not theologically determined worship.

Notices would seem most properly to be part of the movement of response. Having heard God's word read and proclaimed, we now hear about opportunities for ministry and service, hopefully both within the church walls *and* outside during the following week. An alternative case may be made for the notices being part of the gathering, in which case they are being understood as the "family news" when the family of God comes for its weekly "get together." Regardless of which approach is taken, placing the notices somewhere in the middle of the worship service simply doesn't cut it theologically.

As a side note, announcements seem to have a tendency to become ever longer. In part, this often seems to stem from an attempt to use the announcements to try to "sell" congregants—convincing them to join this or that group, activity, or committee or enroll in this or that adult Sunday school class or put more in the offering plate. The pulpit *is not* the place for sales pitches. Give the people of God the facts and then trust the Holy Spirit do his work! Thoughtful use of the bulletin, church website, or overhead screens may also reduce the need for excessively long verbal announcements.

Prayers of the people. Hearing the word of God should drive us to our knees in prayer. We have been in the presence of the one who is altogether holy and awesome. We have heard again the story of God's astonishing love and of his grace (unearned, undeserved favour) toward us. Should we not respond with praise and thanksgiving? Daily life makes it painfully clear that the Kingdom has not yet come in full, that neither our lives nor the world at large are as they should be. Should we not respond by praying for God's broken, suffering, and marred creation and for the inbreaking of the Kingdom in the lives of all people? The prayers of the people should always go well beyond the needs of just the local church, the community, or even the country. "Prayers of the people will always hold up before God whatever brokenness in the world has come to our attention. We pray for victims of natural disasters, disease, warfare, and conflict, for the homeless, and ourselves."[51]

It is often said that the four major elements of prayer are Adoration, Confession, Thanksgiving, and Supplication. (This formula—ACTS—isn't entirely accurate. For example, it leaves out prayers of lament, which are sometimes most appropriate as part of common worship. In a lament, we complain to God that things are not as they ought to be yet continue to express trust in him.) Normally, since confession has happened early in the worship service, it does not form part of the prayers of the people. The prayers of the people therefore usually focus on adoration, thanksgiving, and supplication.

The prayers of the people have a formative aspect—one of the by-products of genuine worship. Such prayers shape and mould us into becoming more and more like Jesus. Adoration (or praise) reminds us regularly of who we are (creatures) in relationship to God (the Creator). Thanksgiving trains us to reject the constant complaining and griping approach to life so common in our culture in favour of a biblical worldview that "forget[s] not all his benefits" (Ps 103:2, AV). The supplication portion of the prayers of the people "opens us to the needs of others and habituates us into the activity of being . . . an intercessor for others. It can develop our empathy for those in pain. Praying for persons and peoples labelled as our enemies changes us by calling into question the way we easily demonize people, groups and countries."[52] This kind of prayer helps shape us into people who are not easily "conned" by depictions in the media or by government that divides the world neatly into "us" who are inevitably good and "them" who are inevitably evil and malicious. Instead, we are constantly reminded that *all* of us are sinners in need of God's grace; *all* of us are wounded and dysfunctional in one way or another. Careful attention to the supplications almost invariably will reveal areas and people who are not on our radar at all. For instance, there may be frequent prayer for pastors and missionaries but almost never any prayer for laypeople whose work, both within and without the church's walls, is just as important. A church that prays together often for natural disasters far away but fails ever to mention, say, the plight of marginalized Aboriginal people in its own country or the teens in ghettoes in its own city needs to think about what is missing in its life as a congregation. A congregation that never prays for political leaders has just as big a problem as one that prays only for those from one political party. Praying for the unsaved but never for economic and social justice and peace is just as incomplete as the opposite proceeding. It is common to hear prayers for those suffering from various physical ailments, but much less common to hear prayers for those struggling with mental illness or dementia. Does that suggest we think mental illness or dementia is shameful or self-inflicted? What does it say to those *in* the congregation who have this kind of illness—that they should keep quiet about it? Do our prayers ever include the unemployed, the underemployed, or those who do not find their jobs very meaningful? What does it say if we never pray for those in prison? That they deserve to be punished and therefore are unworthy of our concern? Do we ever pray for Christians who are trying to bear witness to Christ in the arts—writers, actors, playwrights, filmmakers, painters, dancers, sculptors, and musicians? Failure to do so might mean we don't really think God's writ applies in these areas of life.

It's important to face the reality that it is supplication that often gets the lion's share of time in both personal and corporate prayers. Sometimes our prayers are not much more than a long wish list—"gimme" prayers. Of course the prayers of the people, as a response to God's word, will include a significant amount of praying *for* various things. But the prayers of the people should teach by example and *always* include much time given over to adoration and thanksgiving.

The prayers of the people are to be just that—the prayers of the *people*. They are *not* the people listening in to the prayers of the minister. Consequently, they must *always* use the first person plural (we) and never the first person singular (I). Although on many if not most Sundays it will be the minister who leads these prayers, it is important that they be seen and understood as *truly* the prayers of the people of God. There are many varied ways to accomplish this goal. Obviously a minister who regularly visits his or her people in their homes will be able to include their concerns in prayer. One may include responses for the congregation—"Lord, in your mercy, hear our prayer"—or conclude with a unison praying of the Lord's Prayer. Perhaps it may be appropriate to move from the chancel into the centre aisle, using a wireless microphone, in order to emphasize that it is from *among* the people that the prayers arise. It is also helpful, at least from time to time, for a lay member of the congregation to lead the prayers of the people. A colleague of mine sometimes asks the children of the congregation to write out things for which they are thankful and things about which they are concerned. He then uses these as the basis for the prayers of the people. Another colleague sometimes begins and closes the prayers of the people, but between these two, individuals in the congregation are invited briefly to voice their prayers of praise, thanksgiving, and petition aloud. This approach can be incredibly moving.

Often the prayers of the people may be ended with everyone praying together the Lord's Prayer. It was, after all, the "prayer of the people" that Jesus taught to his disciples at their request. If this approach is taken to conclude the prayers of the people, the transition to the Lord's Prayer may be accomplished smoothly with phrases such as these:

- All these things we ask in the name of Our Lord Jesus Christ, who taught us to pray, saying . . .
- We gather up all our prayers in the prayer Jesus taught to his first followers, saying together . . .

Three final comments are in order about the prayers of the people.

First, there is a widespread attitude among many evangelicals that extemporaneous prayer is somehow evidence of deeper sincerity, or relying more on the Spirit, than is the use of prepared prayer. That is theological nonsense. Who are we to restrict the Holy Spirit? The Spirit can equally move and direct the person carefully preparing a prayer in advance of a worship service as the person who prays without preparation. While it is quite all right to have poorly thought out, stream of consciousness prayers in my private devotions, one needs to ask if this is really acceptable when leading God's people in prayer. Isn't the person leading prayer supposed to be helping the people focus their attention on praying *to* God? When those people are distracted by trying to figure out what the prayer leader is saying as a result of poor grammar or wording, repetitious phrasing, or the repeated use of "Father" or "Lord" as a sort of "filler word" because the leader doesn't know what to say next,[53] they are not as focused on God as they might otherwise be. Unprepared prayers also all too often fall into the habit of focusing almost entirely on petition, thus giving the impression that God is a sort of cosmic bellhop who will "jump to it" whenever we pray, when in fact, the pattern of prayer we need to learn—over and over—is that of submitting ourselves to God utterly and listening for his word to us. Prayers that are unprepared frequently lack balance and fail to be widely inclusive. All of this suggests that at least some degree of preparation is appropriate for anyone who will be leading prayer during common worship.

Second, *all* prayers during common worship need to be biblically and theologically sound—another reason, incidentally, for careful preparation. For instance, far too often prayers in evangelical churches confuse the persons of the Trinity. I am often startled to hear a prayer addressed to "Our Father" that immediately proceeds to "We give you thanks for dying on the cross for us." The Father did not die on the cross—the Son did. On other occasions I've heard prayers addressed to God the Father that are offered "in your precious/holy/wonderful name." Leaving aside the fact that a prayer that makes no mention of Jesus is not explicitly Christian in nature, we are told in Scripture that our access to God is *through* Jesus Christ. The Holy Spirit seems very rarely to be directly addressed, invoked, praised, thanked, or petitioned in the prayers of evangelicals, even though he is just as much Lord and God as the Father and the Son.

Third, the *posture* of prayer is a matter of relative indifference. The fourfold pattern is not concerned with the posture of prayer but with the nature and content of prayer, and with where in an order of service prayer is offered. In some traditions, prayer is offered in the ancient Jewish fashion, standing with arms raised. In other churches worshippers always kneel for prayer, in others one sits with bowed head and perhaps with folded hands. Each of these postures is theologically and biblically defensible. What is appropriate depends on the culture and ethos of a particular congregation.

Offering. Similar to the notices, the offering in evangelical churches often takes place a few moments into the worship service. What this appears to reflect is uncertainty about the meaning of the offering (or lack of thought about its meaning) and a desire to get it over with as quickly as possible, even though "convenience" is most emphatically *not* a theological category!

The offering would seem most properly to be part of the movement of response. In giving our money for the church's work, mission, and ministry, we are responding to God's call and total claim on our lives, a call and claim we have heard *through* the word read and preached. I shall never forget what Miles Keirstead, a retired physics professor in one of the congregations I served, said to me once about the offering. It was, he said, the most important part of the service for him, because in it he could respond to his Lord. The offering, in other words, was where the proverbial rubber met the road, for if a person was serious about following Jesus, that would be reflected in a sacrificial approach to giving. The offering is and should be seen as a profoundly countercultural act. Instead of accepting society's narrative of scarcity and the need for keeping, acquiring, and hoarding, in the offering, I am asserting belief in plentitude and divine generosity. Roger Prentice, long-time chaplain to Acadia University in Nova Scotia, Canada, echoes this understanding: "One of the telltale signs of the seriousness of a congregation's worship is how the Offering is treated in their worship. It is the time when the believer puts his life on the line, and actually gives some of his or her life to God."[54] Prentice further argues that "A tawdry reception and presentation of the offering indicates a very poor understanding of this high act of worship."[55] The offering is not "an incidental part of the service."[56]

The offering is also an opportunity for spiritual formation. This is easily forgotten. When I put a portion of my income onto the offering plate, I am doing more than paying for the church's electric bill, the pastor's salary, or the mission budget. I am, to use the old saying, putting my money where my mouth is. It is one thing to say the right words, quite another to back that with action. Week by week in the offering we are slowly being shaped, slowly learning that the Kingdom is our priority; week by week we are learning that it is in losing/giving away that we add/gain.

Perhaps we also need to widen our understanding of the offering to being more than putting money on an offering plate. Would it be possible, for example, to invite members of the congregation to write out some of the things they are specifically offering to God, or have offered to him in the past week? A lady in the congregation I presently serve regularly places a written note in the offering plate, in addition to her weekly cheque. That note may say things like, "This week I took time to teach the Lord's Prayer to my children" or "This week I spent time every day reading Scripture" or "This week I baked cookies and took some to an elderly neighbour" or "I am going to try to drive more like a Christian this week, not getting angry at other drivers." All of this is part of our offering to God just as much as our financial contributions.

Commissioning. The followers of Jesus have gathered as his family. They have experienced (hopefully) something of the majesty of God, confessed their sins, and listened for God's word to them. That word has prompted them to singing, to prayer, to giving. Now what? Now, the people of God are being sent back out into the wider world, into offices, shops, classrooms, their homes, and countless other situations and places where, very often, Jesus is not accepted as Lord, and the Kingdom needs to break in. Working toward seeing the Kingdom realized is the work of the people—*all* of God's people, outside the church walls, during the next six days. It is outside the walls that there will be opportunities for witness, for speaking a good word for Christ, for inviting others to confess Jesus as Lord. Outside the walls there are people who are hungry and homeless, lonely, addicted, and grieving. Outside the church walls there is political graft, environmental degradation, social and economic injustice. There are systems and structures that are corrupt and that oppress the poor and others. There are unborn children at risk of abortion, terrified pregnant teenagers, elderly pensioners living in dire circumstances, people seeking work, students struggling in school, women being beaten by their male partners, refugees and immigrants trying to find their way and learn a new language. It is *out there* where we must live out our commitment to Christ, and this is particularly true in a secular society. It should be clear that worship is to extend into the new week, and that faith is to be lived out in the context of the home, classroom, office, workshop, and locker room. We leave morning worship to love and serve the Lord Jesus with joy and thanksgiving in the new week, and to make him known by our words and deeds. David L. Stubbs is a Presbyterian minister and Associate Professor of Ethics and Theology at Western Theological Seminary in Michigan. He writes, "the ending of our worship services . . . can help us see if and how our worship is connected to the rest of our lives."[57]

Given all this, it makes good theological sense for the followers of Jesus to be charged or commissioned, week by week, as they are sent out into the world to do the work of the Kingdom, to be Christ's representatives. This sending is especially appropriate since most evangelicals affirm belief in the priesthood of all believers, that is, we believe that *every* Christian is called to be a priest, representing God to humanity and humanity to God. This *isn't* a job *only* for the clergy! So let's actually say this clearly *every* Sunday by commissioning the entire congregation! Such commissioning is a regular reminder of the privilege and extraordinary responsibilities laid upon every Christian. The commissioning can frequently be combined with or immediately followed by the benediction. Here are some sample words of commissioning:

- This service of worship is ended. Yet now our service truly begins. For we return to the world to live out our faith in words and actions.
- You are the people of God (or the followers of Jesus). Go out into this new week to live out the promises you made at your baptisms.
- Go now in peace to love and serve the Lord with joy and thanksgiving.
- The Bible says that the Kingdom of God, that is to say, God's will accomplished, has come only in part. We wait for its fullness when Jesus returns. In the meantime, we are each called to work to see it realized. That is your responsibility and your calling this week.
- We have come here as the gathered church—to worship God, to ask forgiveness and hear words of pardon, to hear God speak to us through Scripture. Now we become the scattered church. We leave this sanctuary, intentionally to live out our faith in Christ in this new week. It is outside these walls where most of the church's work waits for us.[58] "It is where the hurting are helped, the aimless are counseled, the bereaved are comforted, the lost are witnessed to, and the hungry are fed."[59]
- Go out to make Christ known by word and deed in this new week.
- Go from this place to live out your baptismal promises.

Often it will be possible and desirable for the commissioning specifically to reflect the theme of the Scripture lessons and sermon. The minister might choose to write different words of commissioning for every Sunday.

Benediction. The people of God, having been commissioned, are now sent back out into the week, but they are not sent out somehow to manage on their own! They are not sent out alone and cold as it were. No! They are sent out assured of God's ongoing presence and love, with God's blessing ringing in their ears. This blessing is called the benediction (from the Latin *benedictus,* which means blessing).

The benediction is *not* a "closing prayer." It is a blessing, not a prayer. Nor is the benediction the minister blessing the people. Rather it is God's blessing of God's people, through the words of the pastor. Giving the benediction is one of the greatest privileges any pastor has. These are his or her well-loved people, for whose spiritual well-being the pastor will be held accountable by God. The pastor has the astonishing privilege each week of having God speak words of blessing and love over God's people through the pastor's voice. Lee Eclov is the pastor of Village Church of Lincolnshire in Lake Forest, Illinois, an Evangelical Free Church congregation. He penned an article in *Leadership Journal* titled "Let Us Stand for the Benediction: Reclaiming the lost art of blessing." In it Eclov related what a newcomer to the church told him about the benediction: "I've been part of a church . . . as long as I can remember . . . this is the only [one] where the pastor blessed his people. . . . You weren't . . . sending us out to face the world on our own; you were pouring out God's blessing . . . so . . . we would be better prepared to face the world."[60] Is it any wonder that Eclov then wrote, "Benedictions have become one of my favorite pastoral privileges. I can't imagine ending a worship service with, 'See you next week,' or 'You're dismissed,' when I can offer a congregation God's blessing instead."[61]

The benediction is to be brief. Frequently, as a reflection of our theological convictions, it should be Trinitarian in nature. Here is the simple benediction that I use frequently: "Now may the blessing of Almighty God, the Father, the Son, and the Holy Spirit be with you all, this day and forever. Amen." Church history and various different traditions and cultures have also provided us with many different benedictions. Some of these are centuries old and have been hallowed by long use, while others are much more recent. Here are a few examples:

- "May the rich blessing of the Lord attend us, and grant us all remission of sins. May the Lord graciously protect us from all evil and mercifully preserve and keep us in all good, and may He who created and redeemed us preserve us for Himself unspotted to the end. Amen."[62]
- "To Thee, O Master, Lover of men [sic], we have recourse on our departure from Thy sanctuary. May we leave to do Thy work, as we walk kept free from every worldly, evil thing; and from every attack of the evil one, lead us in the way eternal, now and ever and unto ages of ages. Amen."[63]
- "The peace of God, which passeth all understanding, keep your hearts and minds in the knowledge and love of God, and of his Son Jesus Christ our Lord: And the blessing of God Almighty, the Father, the Son and the Holy Ghost, be amongst you and remain with you always. Amen."[64]
- "O Lord, support us all the day long of this troublous life, until the shadows lengthen and the evening comes, the busy world is hushed, the fever of life is over, and our work is done. Then, Lord, in thy mercy, grant us safe lodging, a holy rest, and peace at the last; through Jesus Christ our Lord. Amen."[65]
- "May the peace of the Lord Christ go with you, wherever He may send you. May He guide you through the wilderness, protect you through the storm. May he bring you home rejoicing at the wonders He has shown you. May he bring you home rejoicing once again into our doors. In the name of the Father, and of the Son, and of the Holy Spirit. Amen."[66]

Scripture is of course also a rich source to mine for appropriate benedictions. (Incidentally, given its poetic cadences, this may be one of the few occasions when the words of the Authorized Version may be appropriate for a service of common worship. Normally the antique English is a barrier to understanding.) Here are a few examples:

- "The LORD bless thee and keep thee; the LORD make his face shine upon thee, and be gracious unto thee; the LORD lift up his countenance upon thee and give thee peace" (Num 6:24-26, AV).
- "The LORD shall preserve thee from all evil: he shall preserve thy soul. The LORD shall preserve thy going out and thy coming in from this time forth, and even forever" (Ps 121:7-8, AV).
- "The grace of the Lord Jesus Christ, the love of God, and the communion of the Holy Spirit be with you all" (2 Cor 13:13, AV).
- "The grace of our Lord Jesus Christ be with you all" (Phil 4:23, AV).
- "Now [may] the God of peace, that brought again from the dead our Lord Jesus, that great shepherd of the sheep, through the blood of the everlasting covenant, make you perfect in every good work to do his will, working in you that which is well pleasing in his sight, through Jesus Christ to whom be glory forever and ever. Amen" (Heb 13:20-21, AV).

A Concluding Note: Memorization

Perhaps out of a fear of "rote religion" or "religion of the head but not the heart," many evangelicals are nervous about the idea of memorizing parts of the service of common worship. But "knowing something by heart" does not automatically mean the thing memorized becomes a meaningless recitation. Evangelicals, after all, have often been keen on the practice of memorizing large portions of Scripture—and many parts of common worship are drawn directly from Scripture, the Lord's Prayer probably being the best example. But calls to worship and confession, assurances of pardon, and benedictions also often come directly from Scripture. For centuries, many Christians knew the entire Psalter by heart, in the version they sang daily or weekly during common worship.

"Knowing by heart" other elements of common worship can be a valuable tool for being shaped as followers of Jesus. Short acclamations of praise used regularly—such as the Gloria Patri[67] and the Doxology,[68] shape us theologically as Trinitarians, as people who give praise to God, and as people who know that *all* things come from and belong to God the Creator.

Greetings such as "The Lord be with you . . . And also with you" teach us the "high courtesy of heaven" while answering "Thanks be to God" in response to "This is the word of the Lord" after Scripture is read reminds us that we are *not* just listening to any book but to the very word of God to us. Creeds or confessions of faith help us to set out our convictions in a short, orderly way and, in the case of the ancient, ecumenical creeds, assert our connection with the generations of believers who have gone before us—the faithful departed—who have cherished the same beliefs and hopes.

There is another attractive feature in having parts of common worship that can be memorized over time. These parts allow children to participate more fully in worship with adults. It is astonishingly moving to notice a child, who has been learning the Lord's Prayer in Sunday school, for the first time proudly to be able to join with her parents in that part of the service. It's equally moving to be sitting in front of a teenager who enthusiastically bellows out "Thanks be to God" just a fraction of a second before everyone else after the reading of Scripture.

There is one other argument in favour of what Marva Dawn calls "the value of memorized tradition," for she argues,

> we cannot overstress its importance in this age of transitoriness. Here we are especially concerned for the memory bank of images, theological truths, and doctrinal statements—food for the heart, soul, and mind—that we need to sustain us. If our liturgies incorporate these gifts in such pieces as creeds, psalms, and responses, they provide us with resources for all life.[69]

Surely, in a secular society, surrounded and outnumbered by those who do not share our commitment to following Jesus, indeed often know very little about him, we would be foolish to ignore such resources!

Notes

1. Simon Chan, *Liturgical Theology: The Church as Worshiping Community* (Downers Grove IL: InterVarsity Press, 2006) 53.

2. Christopher J. Ellis, *Approaching God: A Guide for Worship Leaders and Worshippers* (Norwich: Canterbury Press, 2009) 34.

3. Precisely *why* God refused Cain's offering is not explained.

4. J. Daniel Day, *Seeking the Face of God: Evangelical Worship Reconceived* (Macon GA: Nurturing Faith, 2013) 6–7.

5. Thomas G. Long, *Beyond the Worship Wars: Building Vital and Faithful Worship* (Herdon VA: The Alban Institute, 2001) 87.

6. Ibid.

7. Carrie Titcombe Steenwyk and John D. Witvliet, eds., *The Worship Sourcebook*, 2nd ed. (Grand Rapids MI: Calvin Institute of Christian Worship, Faith Alive Christian Resources, Baker Books, 2013) 24, emphasis added.

8. The earliest description of a Christian worship service outside the New Testament is that of Justin Martyr, about the year AD 150. It clearly follows the fourfold "catholic" pattern.

9. R. Kent Hughes, "Free Church Worship: The Challenge of Freedom," in *Worship by the Book*, ed. D. A. Carson (Grand Rapids MI: Zondervan, 2002) 147.

10. Robert E. Webber, *Worship Is a Verb: Celebrating God's Mighty Deeds of Salvation* (Peabody MA: Hendrickson, 2004) 5–6.

11. Annie Dillard, *Teaching a Stone to Talk: Expeditions and Encounters* (New York: Harper Perennial, 1992) 52–53.

12. Webber, *Worship Is a Verb*, 142.

13. Robert G. Rayburn, *O Come, Let Us Worship: Corporate Worship in the Evangelical Church* (Grand Rapids MI: Baker Book House, 1980; repr., Eugene OR: Wipf and Stock, 2010) 174.

14. John Jefferson Davis, *Worship and the Reality of God: An Evangelical Theology of Real Presence* (Downers Grove IL: InterVarsity Press, 2010) 102–103.

15. Long, *Beyond the Worship Wars*, viii.

16. John D. Witvliet, "The Opening of Worship: Trinity," in *A More Profound Alleluia: Theology and Worship in Harmony*, ed. Leanne Van Dyk, in the Calvin Institute of Christian Worship Liturgical Studies Series (hereafter "Calvin Institute Series"), ed. John D. Witvliet (Grand Rapids MI: Eerdmans, 2005) 12.

17. The Iona Community, *Iona Abbey Worship Book* (Glasgow: Wild Goose Publications, 2001) 75.

18. *The Book of Worship for Church and Home: with orders of worship, services for the administration of the sacraments and other aids to worship according to the usages of the Methodist Church* (Nashville: The Methodist Publishing House, 1965) 180.

19. Church Then and Now: The Masai Creed, http:/churchthenandnow.com/2009/10/29 (accessed 8 June 2013).

20. Edwin Arrison, Kairos Southern Africa: An Anti-poverty Creed, http://kairossouthernafrica.wordpress.com/2011/06/03/an-anti-poverty-creed/ (accessed 8 June 2013).

21. "CNI Mission Statement," Church of North India: 44 Years of United Witness & Service, www.cnisynod.org (accessed 25 September 2015).

22. Martin Luther, "Deutsche Messe, 1526," in *Liturgies of the Western Church*, ed. Bard Thompson (Philadelphia: Fortress, 1988) 123–40.

23. Ulrich Zwingli, "Liturgy of the Word, 1525," in *Liturgies of the Western Church*, ed. Thompson, 147–48.

24. Martin Bucer, "Psalter, with Complete Church Practice," in *Liturgies of the Western Church*, ed. Thompson, 167–81.

25. John Calvin, "The Form of Church Prayers, Strassburg, 1545, & Geneva, 1542," in *Liturgies of the Western Church*, ed. Thompson, 185–210, 216–24.

26. John Knox, "The Forme of Prayers," in *Liturgies of the Western Church*, ed. Thompson, 295–310.

27. Balthasar Hubmaier, "On Fraternal Admonition," "A Form of Water Baptism," "A Form for Christ's Supper," in *Balthasar Hubmaier: Theologian of Anabaptism*, ed. and trans. H. Wayne Pipkin and John H. Yoder, vol. 5 in Classics of the Radical Reformation, ed. Cornelius J. Dyck (Kitchener, Ontario: Herald Press, 1989) 372–408.

28. William A. Dyrness, "Confession and Assurance: Sin and Grace," *A More Profound Alleluia*, ed. Van Dyk, in Calvin Institute Series, ed. Witvliet, 45.

29. Ibid., 41.

30. Robert Benson, *Living Prayer* (New York: Tarcher/Penguin, 1998) 24.

31. Dyrness, "Confession and Assurance," 38.

32. Davis, *Worship and the Reality of God*, 103.

33. In many evangelical churches, it is not at all unusual to go for many months without hearing a single word read from the Hebrew Scriptures, effectively making us latter-day Marcionites. Marcion (died c. AD 160) was a heretic, formally excommunicated by the early church. Marcion rejected the Old Testament entirely. His canon of Scripture included only ten of Paul's letters and an edited version of Luke's Gospel.

34. Ellis, *Approaching God*, 105.

35. Being a human creation, no lectionary of course is ever "perfect," and the Revised Common Lectionary is no exception. For example, one of the major criticisms of the RCL is that it omits large parts of the Old Testament. While this is true, in many evangelical churches, switching to the use of the RCL would *still* result in vastly increasing the amount read from the Old Testament. Moreover, many of the passages not read from the Old Testament according to the RCL pattern are lengthy genealogies, lists detailing numbers such as the number of men from this or that tribe who are part of an army, verses repeated word for word (or almost word for word) in other books of the Old Testament, or passages from books such as Leviticus with its highly detailed instructions pertaining to ritual purity, animal sacrifices, and the like. While these are all unquestionably part of Scripture, I am reminded of the words of my seminary homiletics professor, Dr. Harold L. Mitton: "all Scripture is inspired, but some parts are more inspiring than others!"

36. Very often a person who is not good at reading Scripture aloud may be taught this skill. This does however require *deliberate* teaching and coaching.

37. Ellis, *Approaching God*, 109.

38. Tim Suttle, *Shrink: Faithful Ministry in a Church-Growth Culture* (Grand Rapids MI: Zondervan, 2014) 207.

39. Marva J. Dawn, *Reaching Out without Dumbing Down: A Theology of Worship for This Urgent Time* (Grand Rapids MI: Eerdmans, 1995) 238, emphasis added.

40. An excellent introduction to both exegesis and hermeneutics is Gordon D. Fee and Douglas Stuart, *How to Read the Bible for All Its Worth* (Grand Rapids MI: Zondervan, 1982; repr., Grand Rapids MI: Zondervan, 2003).

41. Robert Smith, Jr., *Doctrine that Dances: Bringing Doctrinal Preaching and Teaching to Life* (Nashville: B & H, 2008) 25.

42. Michael Horton, *A Better Way: Rediscovering the Drama of God-Centered Worship* (Grand Rapids MI: Baker, 2003) 57, 60.

43. M. Craig Barnes, *The Pastor as Minor Poet: Texts and Subtexts in the Ministerial Life*, in Calvin Institute Series, ed. Witvliet (Grand Rapids MI: Eerdmans, 2009) 9.

44. Ibid., 18.

45. https://en.wikipedia.org/wiki/Death_and_funeral_of_Otto_von_Habsburg

46. Mention should be made at this point of the widespread practice of permanently displaying national flags in church sanctuaries or flying the national flag on a flagpole outside the church building. This is a highly questionable practice that supports the mindset of Constantinian Christianity, confusing "my country" with loyalty to Jesus Christ. At the very least this practice sends distinctly mixed messages: Who or what has pre-eminence for followers of Jesus Christ? Is there ever a situation where loyalty to Christ means opposing one's country? Is a person who is a follower of Jesus but not a citizen of the country whose flag is displayed fully welcome?

47. Edward H. Hammett, *The Gathered and Scattered Church: Equipping Believers for the 21st Century* (Macon GA: Smyth & Helwys, 1999) 13.

48. Ibid., 15.

49. Although this book focuses on common worship *exclusive* of the sacraments of Baptism and Holy Communion, it should at least be noted that the appropriate place for both, since they both contain strong elements of response to God, is toward the end of a worship service.

50. The Apostle Paul wrote to the Ephesians of "sing[ing] psalms and hymns and spiritual songs" (Eph 5:19, AV). Similarly he encouraged the Colossians, "with gratitude in your hearts sing psalms, hymns and spiritual songs to God" (Col 3:16). Pliny the Younger was the Roman governor of Bithynia-Pontus (in modern-day Turkey). Reporting in a letter dated about AD 112 to the Emperor Trajan about the Christians in his district, Pliny observed that it was the custom of the Christians when they gathered to sing "an anthem to Christ as to God."

51. Ronald P. Byars, "Creeds and Prayers: Ecclesiology," *A More Profound Alleluia*, ed. Van Dyk, in Calvin Institute Series, ed. Witvliet, 103.

52. David L. Stubbs, "Ending of Worship: Ethics," *A More Profound Alleluia*, ed. Van Dyk, in Calvin Institute Series, ed. Witvliet, 145.

53. This practice is tantamount to a violation of the third commandment, which requires that we take God's name seriously. Using God's name as a way to fill up otherwise "dead air" does not seem to be taking God, or his name, very seriously.

54. Roger H. Prentice, *Hymns at Heaven's Gate: The Use & Abuse of Hymns* (Kentville, N.S.: Gaspereau Press, 2008) 36–37.

55. Ibid., 11.

56. Ibid.

57. Stubbs, "Ending of Worship: Ethics," in *A More Profound Alleluia*, ed. Van Dyk, Calvin Institute Series, ed. Witvliet, 134.

58. Hammett, *The Gathered and Scattered Church*, 13.

59. Ibid.

60. Lee Eclov, "Let Us Stand for the Benediction: Reclaiming the lost art of blessing," *Leadership Journal*, Winter 2009, http://www.christianitytoday.com/le/2009/winter/letusstandbenediction.html (accessed 25 September 2015).

61. Ibid.

62. This benediction is from the Mozarabic Psalter. List composed by W. A. (Wip) Martin, "Benedictions from Various Sources," http://rockhay.tripod.com/worship/benewip.htm (accessed 8 June 2013).

63. This benediction is adapted from the Prayer of St. Makarius the Great and is taken from the Russian Orthodox Prayer Book. Found at http://rockhay.tripod.com/worship/benewip.htm (accessed 8 June 2013).

64. From the Anglican Church of Canada, *The Book of Common Prayer* (Cambridge: Cambridge University Press, 1962) 86.

65. Ibid., 58.

66. From the Northumbria Community, *Celtic Daily Prayer* (London: Harper Collins, 2000) 19.

67. The Gloria Patri is so named after the first opening words in Latin—Glory be to the Father. "Glory be to the Father and to the Son and to the Holy Ghost. As it was in the beginning, is now and ever shall be, world without end. Amen. Amen." Christians have used this ascription of praise for approximately 1,700 years. Initially it was a means of affirming belief in the Trinity, over against the Arian heresy of the 300s that denied the full deity of both Jesus and the Holy Spirit. Customarily, it is sung *after* the psalm but *before* any readings from the New Testament, thus emphasizing that the God revealed in the Old Testament is the same as the one revealed in the New, and made known to us best in Jesus, who was God come among us.

68. The words of the doxology most commonly used among Protestants were written by Thomas Ken in 1674: "Praise God from whom all blessings flow, Praise him all creatures here below, Praise him above ye heavenly host, Praise Father, Son, and Holy Ghost. Amen." The doxology is frequently used as a short hymn of praise after the offering has been presented.

69. Dawn, *Reaching Out without Dumbing Down*, 259–60.

Chapter 5

Music and Common Worship

The people of God have long been a singing people: Miriam sang a song after Israel escaped Pharaoh's army, Moses taught a song to the people, the entire book of psalms is a collection of songs, the temple in Jerusalem had temple singers, the apostles say to "sing psalms, hymns and spiritual songs to God" (Col 3:16c), and even John's revelation describes music. Music appears repeatedly in the Bible. In modern Western society music is a powerful and enormously influential force. "Individuals define themselves according to the music that they listen to . . . movements create songs to represent their goals and aspirations, and advertisers use music to sell their products and create brand loyalty."[1] The power of music is something that Christians in general and evangelicals in particular have long known. We humans are not disembodied minds. We were created with physical bodies and minds, bodies and souls united, and Jesus taught that our first duty was to love God with our hearts, minds, souls, and strength—in other words, with our *entire* beings. The worship of God is not restricted to a few aspects of our humanity; rather our worship of God is to involve us entirely. The stories of creation, in which God deems all he has created as "good," the incarnation when God becomes a physical human being in Jesus, his own *physical* resurrection and the hope of our own resurrection, should make it clear that God not only has no problem with but in fact positively rejoices in physicality. Worship therefore both can and should include the physical—and that preeminently means music.

What is the role of music in common worship? How can music be used for the worship of God, particularly in the evangelical tradition? Can music be secularized and contribute to a secular worldview, or is music value neutral? All of these are important questions.

Music

Music has been called "the war department of the church." Countless battles have been waged within local congregations about music styles. Tragically, these conflicts have often shown Christians at their worst, ascribing (frequently false) devious motives to others, being ungracious, unloving, and unkind, demanding their own way, complaining, backbiting, and gossiping. If all this were not bad enough, often such conflicts are based not on matters theological or biblical but merely on different aesthetic preferences on the part of the combatants. Let's be clear about this! Different people have different aesthetic preferences when it comes to music (or any of the arts for that matter). However, *aesthetic preferences different from one's own must not be automatically equated with bad theology or bad worship.* I have attended worship services the music of which I found irritating, even grating to my aesthetic sensibilities, *but* the worship service itself was theologically informed and shaped, reflected the fourfold biblical pattern, incorporated the distinctive evangelical emphases, and clearly did not foster but challenged the secular approach to life. Whatever I may have felt about the music was, frankly, irrelevant. Biblically shaped, theologically sound genuine worship was happening. *That* is what was important.

The Relationship of Music and Word

For Protestant Christians in general and evangelicals in particular, the preeminence of Scripture means that the role of music in common worship is to support the message of the word, both read (i.e., the Bible) and proclaimed (i.e., the sermon). As R. Kent Hughes writes, "music must principally serve the text."[2] Just as it is axiomatic in Protestant theology that word precedes (and explains) sacrament, so also word precedes (and explains) music. Without the word, music either has nothing to say or is ambiguous. On the other hand, the message of the word supported by music may be better communicated than without, and may well reach the affective aspect of individuals in ways that are not otherwise easily engaged. The key however is that whether it be a minister of music, choir member, organist, choir director, soloist, or instrumentalist, "Musicians must see themselves as fellow laborers in the Word."[3] Music for common worship must be biblically solid, with a clear and sound theological and doctrinal foundation. Common worship is not about merely getting our doctrine right, but it should not be about less than that either.

The Function of Music in Common Worship

What role does music have in common worship? Under the overall rubric of supporting the word, what is it supposed to do? Sometimes it is easier to explain or define something by explaining first what it is not. This is the case with the role of music in worship.

First, music should never be an opportunity for showcasing talent to the congregation. A congregation is not an "audience" and should neither be thought of nor referred to as such. Words matter, and the word "audience" reveals a profoundly secularized idea of what worship is about. An audience comes expecting to be entertained by experts, by people they have paid to see. Once they disperse, the members of an audience have no ties to one another and no common goal toward which they are working. A Christian congregation gathers as a community of people who have relationships with one another that extend beyond the service of common worship. A congregation gathers for worship to focus on God, to worship, adore, praise, and thank God, to seek God's forgiveness, to hear God's words and to respond to them. Its common goal, whether at common worship or during the week, is seeing the Kingdom of God realized. A congregation usually has leaders, but they are not there to entertain and the focus is not on them. Rather, such leaders help direct everyone's attention to God. (This incidentally raises a question about the widespread practice of applauding after musical pieces during common worship. It's doubtful if those applauding imagine they are clapping for God! And if they are in fact indicating their approval or support of the efforts of the musician[s] they are, by definition, no longer focused on God.) In one sense the perfect piece of music (or sermon) in common worship would be a piece of music (or sermon) that makes people forget what is happening because the music (or sermon) so completely leads them into the presence of God that everything else drops away. This being so, music must never be a "performance." Instead, it is, as a colleague describes it, "a *gift* of music," the gift being offered *by* the musician(s) first to God and second to God's people as a tool for *their* offering themselves completely to God.

Second, music is not to be used in a mantric fashion. Buddhism, Hinduism, Sikhism, and Jainism encourage followers to repeat the same word or words endlessly as a means of emptying the mind in order to find truth or unity with the "one." Music that appears to be aiming at putting everyone into an almost trance-like, empty-minded state has no place in Christian common worship. Jesus did not want empty heads but heads rightly filled and minds that worshipped God. Truth was revealed, made known, not wrested from an unwilling deity who was trying to hide.

What positive roles then does music have in common worship—beyond supporting the word, which is its primary role?

First, music is "to engage [the congregation] at the affective level so that their whole beings . . . are caught up in wonder, love and praise of God."[4] Certainly the word can and will engage our emotions, but music can also deepen and enhance that engagement. The 1975 blockbuster film *Jaws* was the story of a giant, person-eating great white shark that started attacking beachgoers in a fictional summer resort town. I remember seeing a clip from which the musical score had been removed. It made a remarkable difference. Of course one knew that dreadful things were going to happen, but without the buildup of the famous theme music, with only the narrative, the movie was rather dull and unengaging. While the word can and does engage our emotions, when word is supported by music, our affective side can often be much more fully involved than otherwise.

Second, music is a kind of "spiritual nourishment."[5] Whether preachers like to admit it or not, much of the theology by which laypeople function in day-to-day life is communicated through hymns and choruses. That is one reason why the choice of music and the work of musicians are so important. More still, even at the end of life "When . . . we . . . can remember little else, we are still likely to recall the songs learned in childhood. Music has the uncanny ability to burrow its way into our spiritual bones. When it comes to matters of spirituality and faith, we are what we sing."[6]

Third, music is a means by which all the fourfold parts of worship may be expressed by God's people. Most obvious of course is praise. Likely the majority of hymns and choruses are songs of praise, thanksgiving, and adoration. But music can also be a vehicle for expression of godly sorrow and repentance. Consider for example the penitential psalms,[7] notably Psalm 51, attributed to King David after he was confronted by the prophet Nathan. A good many "gospel hymns" also include expressions of repentance for sin. It has long been known to preachers—whether they like to admit it or not is another question—that much of the theology and biblical knowledge members of their congregations operate with comes from well-loved, oft-sung hymns and choruses rather than from sermons. Hymns and choruses can teach Scripture and important theological concepts—which is one reason it is so critical to choose pieces that teach accurately. Music can also motivate us to respond to the word. On many Sundays, the hymn of response will strike an upbeat, triumphant note as God's people are sent back out into the world to be agents of the Kingdom.

Fourth, music can be a way for a congregation, made up of many different individuals, to speak with one voice. Part of the deep message of the story of the Tower of Babel is that humanity's sin has not only driven us apart from God but also from one another. We can no longer speak with one voice because our individual voices are not focused on the praise of God. The Pentecost story is about Babel—the effects of sin—being reversed. The disciples, focused on the God they have come to know so well in Jesus, speak with one voice praising God, and once more all can understand. The Protestant Reformers were quite right when they insisted on returning music to *all* the people of God. Singing was not to be restricted to a choir or to chanting priests. So today, music should not be restricted to a "praise and worship" team that sings while the people largely are silent, unable to join in pieces that are unfamiliar or unsuitable for congregational singing. (This does not mean praise and worship teams or choirs do not have a place. They do, but that place is not to sing on behalf of or instead of God's people as a whole!)

Secularization of Music

Music is not value neutral. It says something. The question is whether that something being said supports, models, and conveys a biblical worldview in which God is central or a secular worldview in which God is unimportant to and at the edges of day-to-day life. *All* music—regardless of lyrics—says *something*. It tells a story of some kind. I once introduced a teenager whose tastes were for heavy metal, rock, and jazz to the music, without lyrics, of Handel's coronation anthem "Zadok, the Priest." Then I asked him what he thought it was about. His response: "something important, something majestic is happening." He had no idea that the piece he had heard had been composed for the coronation of King George II in 1727, and has been used at the coronation of every British monarch since. But he still was able to articulate what the music was saying. Of course, once lyrics are added, a piece of music says something—tells a story—that much more clearly.

Secularization happens most obviously when the lyrics of hymns, songs, or choruses are directed not to God but instead concentrate on the feelings, situation, or experience of worshippers, or sometimes on our desire for self-realization or improvement in one way or another. Whether hymn, song, or chorus, the motion of music in common worship should be toward *God*, not the worshipper. Lyrics that are heavily tilted toward the use of words such as "I," "me," "our," or "we" should therefore be used sparingly, if at all. When such lyrics are used, it is preferable that they at least focus on the community of faith, the church, using the first person plural ("we") rather than the first person singular ("I").

But a question also needs to be raised—apart from lyrics—as to whether some *styles or genres* of music are largely incompatible with Christian common worship, whether some styles are mainly innately secular in nature. For example, "the discordance and dissonance of much 'heavy metal' and such music . . . seems to portray a confused, chaotic, lost world that is in direct contrast to the Christian message of beauty, harmony and spiritual peace."[8] Questions about style and genre are much more difficult to consider than lyrics, but they do matter.

Selecting Music for Common Worship

Several important principles derived from our understanding of what Scripture says is the nature and pattern of worship should be kept in mind when choosing music for common worship. Hymns or choruses should rarely if ever be chosen *only* because they are well liked. The worship of God is not about a "Top 40" list, not even a "Top 40" list of hymns or choruses.

First, all music needs to pass this test: Is the content worthwhile? Do the lyrics say something that is both important and scriptural? Any piece of music that fails this test should not be used at all, whether as a congregational hymn, a choir or solo piece, or even in private worship. Music is never to be chosen based on its popularity: for Protestants in general and evangelicals in particular, word must judge music *not* the other way around.

Second, music should be chosen so that it comes in the right sequence. In other words, it should align with whichever of the four elements of worship is happening during which the music occurs. A hymn of repentance is not normally what would begin a service of worship (though that might be appropriate for an Ash Wednesday or Good Friday service). Instead, a hymn or song of praise or praise choruses normally come at the beginning of a service of worship. Similarly, hymns that are much more obviously about responding to God and being sent back into the wider world belong at the end of the service, not the middle or beginning.

Third, music should also revolve around the major theme of the service—determined by the word. For example, if the Scripture texts and sermon are about stewardship of the environment, the hymn of praise or chorus should probably lead worshippers to praising and thanking God for God's marvelous creation, while the concluding hymn or chorus might include lyrics that speak of the Christian commitment to caring for God's world.

Fourth, if the intention is that a piece will be sung by the congregation, the piece must actually be within the ability of ordinary, musically untrained people who cannot read music. Most emphatically, this *does not* mean that no new hymns or choruses are ever to be introduced to a congregation. With careful introduction, this is both desirable and possible. (A new piece of music may first appear as an instrumental piece, then sung by a group as an anthem, and finally by the entire congregation.) However, the people of God should not be robbed of participation in worship through having pieces that require trained singing skills or the ability to read music.

Fifth, in selecting music it is important to distinguish between "hymns" and "songs" and know what each of these two forms can best accomplish. Hymns tend

> to have a number of verses and the train of thought is a linear one. This means that ideas are developed through the hymn such that where you end up is a different place from where you have started. This will usually mean that the logic of the words do not work well if you were to repeat parts, or all, of the hymn. Instead, the words take you on a journey from the opening statement to the closing action.[9]

On the other hand,

> a song lends itself to repetition. A song will tend to have only one idea, but one which can be impressed on the minds of the singers through repetition. While the linear thought of a hymn lends itself to storytelling, or the development of a theological idea, the simple repetition of a song offers the opportunity for intensification.[10]

Using this explanation, gospel "hymns," which tend to have a refrain repeated after each stanza, and choruses are both in the song category, while "standard hymns" (usually no refrain) fall into the hymn category. When choosing a piece of music, one needs to ask if that part of the worship service is best supported by a hymn or a song.

Finally, context is always important in choosing music. The kind of music that helps people in an inner-city ghetto church worship God may not fulfil that function adequately, if at all, for those attending worship in a Gothic cathedral. The "gospel hymns" that strongly support the word in a country church probably will not do an especially good job of that in a suburban church where most of those gathered for worship have never been on a farm or ranch. Always remember: "Music is a means to an end and we must never lose sight of that end—helping people to worship God. If music gets in the way—then get rid of the music!"[11] Or to be more precise, get rid of the music that has gotten in the way of worship for the people in a particular context and replace it with music that does help those people worship God.

Music Resources

I have found a number of resources particularly helpful in selecting hymns and songs that can support the fourfold biblical pattern of worship, are faithful to the historic evangelical emphases, and promote a biblical rather than secular worldview:

- *Carolyn Winfrey Gillette.* Rev. Carolyn Gillette is an extraordinarily gifted Presbyterian minister who co-pastors Limestone Presbyterian Church in Wilmington, Delaware. She has written lyrics to dozens of new hymns using familiar, well-known hymn tunes. Many of these hymns are Scripture stories or events set to music. Other hymns focus on contemporary events, crises, and concerns, ranging from Hurricane Mitch (that devastated Honduras, Nicaragua, and El Salvador in 1998) and 9/11 (the bombings of September 11, 2001, in the United States) to environmental stewardship, peacemaking, racism, war, health, and hunger. Carolyn has also penned a sung prayer of confession, and sung versions of both the Lord's Prayer and the Apostles' Creed. Gillette's website is <www.carolynshymns.com>. She has published two collections of her hymns: *Gifts of Love: New Hymns for Today's Worship* (Louisville: Geneva Press, 2000) and *Songs of Grace: New Hymns for God and Neighbor* (Nashville: Discipleship Resources, 2009).
- *For the Living of These Days.* Similar to Gillette's work, this volume contains lyrics to many new hymns that use familiar, well-known hymn tunes. Also included are short litanies and prayers. See C. Michael Hawn, *For the Living of These Days: Resources for Enriching Worship* (Macon GA: Smyth & Helwys, 1995).
- *Cyberhymnal.* The cyberhymnal is found at <www.hymntime.com>. With close to 10,000 standard hymns and gospel songs, this site also provides lyrics, sheet music, and biographies of authors and composers. Each hymn or song has a midi audio file—very helpful for those who cannot sight-read or do so only with difficulty. Indexes allow searches by titles of music and scores, Scripture allusions, tunes by name and metre, and topic.

In many cases, alternate tunes are suggested for the hymn, chorus, or song one is considering.

- *Iona Community.* The Iona Community was established by the Reverend George MacLeod (from 1967 Baron MacLeod of Fuinary) in 1938 as a project to narrow the gap he perceived between the established (Presbyterian) Church of Scotland and the needs of working-class people in Glasgow who were suffering greatly as a result of the Great Depression. MacLeod, together with a group of clergy and working men, began rebuilding the ruined medieval Benedictine abbey on the island of Iona. The community eventually loosened its ties with the Church of Scotland in order to become more ecumenical in nature, welcoming women and men from many different walks of life and from many traditions of the Christian church, as well as seekers with no faith commitment. Although many of its activities take place at the Iona Abbey, the Community's headquarters are in Glasgow, which is also where its publishing house, Wild Goose Publications, is based. Part of the community's mission is the renewal of worship, with particular emphasis on Celtic Christianity. Wild Goose Publications (<www.ionabooks.com>) has an extensive list of songbooks as well as CDs, DVDs, and MP3s. Many of these songs and hymns are the work of John Bell and the Wild Goose Resource Group. These include contemporary settings for psalms, hymns for different seasons of the church calendar, and pieces celebrating God's creation and reflecting Christian commitments to peace, the environment, and justice.
- *Northumbria Community.* Like Iona, the Northumbria Community draws deeply from the heritage of Celtic Christianity. Established in 1990, members of the Community are dispersed worldwide, with a Mother House, named "Nether Springs," in Northumberland, England. In addition to a multitude of worship resources, including the excellent *Celtic Daily Prayer* (London: HarperCollins, 2000), members of the community have produced a number of hymns and worship songs. The website for the community is <www.northumbriacommunity.org>.
- *Taizé Community.* The Taizé Community was founded in France during the Second World War by Roger Schütz, a Swiss citizen. It is an ecumenical monastic order, with brothers from both the Protestant and Roman Catholic branches of Christianity. Every year tens of thousands of young people make pilgrimages to Taizé for prayer, Scripture study, and work. The community has been involved in humanitarian work—providing food, supporting education, and assisting in medical care in places as diverse as South Sudan, North Korea, Ethiopia, and Cambodia.

The community has been widely lauded by both Protestants and Roman Catholics for its ecumenical emphasis and its encouragement of a lifestyle that focuses on simplicity, kindness, and reconciliation. The community has developed a worldwide reputation for its musical composition, with simple words or phrases frequently drawn directly from the Bible, especially the Psalms. The music is often meditative in nature. The website, which includes information about both books and recordings, is <www.taize.fr/en>.

- *Judson Concordance to Hymns.* Although currently out of print, this extremely helpful reference volume can sometimes be purchased second-hand. It indexes each line of over 2,300 hymns by key word, enabling the user to identify the hymn if she or he can recall any line of any stanza. See Thomas B. McDormand and Frederic S. Crossman, *Judson Concordance to Hymns* (1965; repr., Valley Forge PA: Judson Press, 1975).

- *Psalter.*[12] The *Scottish Metrical Psalter: Psalms of David in Metre* (Point Roberts WA: Eremitical Press, 2007) is an inexpensive paperback edition of the Scottish Metrical Psalter that has been in continuous use since first published in 1650. Almost all of the psalms are set to Common Metre 8.6.8.6. and can therefore easily be sung to a variety of widely known standard hymn tunes including AMAZING GRACE, ANTIOCH, AZMON, CORONATION, CRIMOND, DIADEM, DUMFERLINE, IRISH, MARTYRDOM, RICHMOND, ST. AGNES, ST. ANNE, ST. FLAVIAN, ST. MAGNUS, and SALZBURG. A useful contemporary psalter, co-published in 2012 by the Calvin Institute of Christian Worship, Faith Alive Christian Resources, and Brazos Press is *Psalms for All Seasons: A Complete Psalter for Worship*. All 150 psalms are set to music—often well-known hymns or folk tunes. As well there are appendices providing specific helps for guitar players.

- *Graham Kendrick.* Graham Kendrick is a prolific English songwriter. Among his more well-known pieces are "The Feast" and "Shine Jesus Shine." Although some of his pieces include somewhat repetitive lyrics, there is both emotional and theological depth to his work. See <www.grahamkendrick.co.uk>.

- *Timothy Dudley-Smith.* Timothy Dudley-Smith is a retired Church of England bishop who is responsible for hundreds of new hymns. His best-known piece is likely "Tell Out My Soul," a paraphrase of the Magnificat. Frequently set to well-known hymn tunes, Dudley-Smith's hymns reflect his evangelical Anglican heritage. See <www.timothydudley-smith.com>.

- *Stuart Townend.* Stuart Townend, the son of a Church of England clergyman, is another English hymn writer. His hymns have both theological depth and a notably poetic quality. His best-known compositions include "In Christ Alone," "The Power of the Cross," and "Resurrection Hymn."

A Note on Metre

By no means is every minister or worship leader able to sight-read music. It is clearly an advantage to be able to do so, but for those who cannot read music or who read slowly or with difficulty, there is a simple way to determine if a set of lyrics will fit any particular tune that you know is familiar to the congregation.

Almost every hymnbook contains an index giving the metre for each hymn. The metre is in the form of a number, for example: 8.6.8.6. The metre simply indicates the number of syllables for the lines in each stanza of the hymn. Knowing the metre allows for marrying lyrics with an appropriate tune.

For example, suppose a minister is preaching on the subject of the second coming of Christ and decides that the lyrics of the hymn "Lo, He Comes with Clouds Descending" will strongly support the focus of his or her sermon. But what if the tune provided in many hymnbooks (HELMSLEY) is completely foreign to his or her congregation, or beyond its ability? Checking the metre of "Lo, He Comes," the minister discovers it is 87.87.87. Knowing this, she or he can then match the lyrics with the tune of *any* other hymn that has the same metre. Thus "Lo, He Comes with Clouds Descending" may *also* be sung to the tunes LAUDA ANIMA ("Praise, My Soul the King of Heaven") and REGENT SQUARE ("Christ Is Made the Sure Foundation").

Many hymns will simply list the metre as "C.M." (Common Metre), which is 8.6.8.6, or "L.M." (Long Metre), which is 8.8.8.8. The lyrics of any hymn with a common metre will normally fit the tune of any hymn using common metre; the lyrics of any hymn with a long metre will normally fit the tune of any hymn using long metre.

Notes

1. C. Randall Bradley, "Music as Liturgy," in *Gathering Together: Baptists at Work in Worship*, ed. Rodney Wallace Kennedy, Derek C. Hatch (Eugene OR: Wipf and Stock, 2013) 131.

2. R. Kent Hughes, "Free Church Worship: The Challenge of Freedom," in *Worship by the Book*, ed. D. A. Carson (Grand Rapids MI: Zondervan, 2002) 167.

3. Ibid., 171.

4. Ben Witherington III, *We Have Seen His Glory: A Vision of Kingdom Worship*, in Calvin Institute of Christian Worship Liturgical Studies Series, ed. John D. Witvliet (Grand Rapids MI: Eerdmans, 2010) 17.

5. John D. Witvliet, *Worship Seeking Understanding: Windows into Christian Practice* (Grand Rapids MI: Baker, 2013) 234.

6. Ibid., 231.

7. The penitential psalms, which express sorrow for sins committed, are generally considered to be Psalms 6, 32, 38, 51, 102, 130 and 143.

8. Roger H. Prentice, *Hymns at Heaven's Gate: The Use & Abuse of Hymns* (Kentville, N.S.: Gaspereau Press, 2008) 31.

9. Christopher J. Ellis, *Approaching God: A Guide for Worship Leaders and Worshippers* (Norwich: Canterbury Press, 2009) 88.

10. Ibid., 90.

11. Ibid., 85.

12. N. T. Wright makes a powerful case for a much more robust use of the psalms in worship in *The Case for the Psalms: Why They are Essential* (New York: HarperCollins, 2013). He argues that regular uses of the psalms "gently but firmly transform our understandings . . . in order that we may be changed, transformed, so that we look at the world, one another, and ourselves in a radically different way, which we believe to be God's way" (7). The psalms not only serve a formational purpose but also, believes Wright, help us truly to be countercultural people: "when the psalms do their work in us and through us, they should equip us the better to live by and promote that alternative worldview" (19).

Chapter 6

Resources for Common Worship that Is Not Secularized

What happens during common worship on Sunday mornings is important. Why? Because common worship is one of the four circles of worship mentioned at the outset of this book, and each of those four circles brings us face to face with the most important issue of all:

> The ultimate issue in human history is . . . *Who shall humans worship?* They waver between true worship and its moral ethos on one end of the spectrum and idolatry and immorality on the other end. . . . Why is this the ultimate issue in life . . . ? Because human beings were created for worship of course. It is that which is the aim and purpose of human beings at the end of the day: to recognize and celebrate their creaturehood by recognizing that only God is God and they are not. . . . Worship is where the creation is finally in order.[1]

For those who are serious about doing common worship better, in ways that are faithful to both the fourfold biblical pattern and the historic evangelical emphases, ways that challenge rather than foster a secular approach to life, there are many practical resources available. Some are ancient and involve returning to some of the tried and tested practices of the early and sub-apostolic church. Other resources are as contemporary as the Internet. This concluding chapter is a highly selective listing and discussion of just a few of these practical resources.

The Church Calendar

For many evangelicals the church calendar is virtually unknown. Often there is a vague understanding that Anglicans/Episcopalians, Lutherans, Roman Catholics, and some others have a variety of observations that are part of their tradition, but for many evangelicals the only recurring observations from year to year are Christmas and Easter.

What Is the Church Calendar?

Simply put, the church calendar is a distinctively Christian way of marking or counting the days and seasons of the year. It is, in effect, an aid to seeking to make God first in daily life. The church calendar uses the same 365 days of the year as the civil/secular calendar we use every day to set up doctor's appointments, record birthdays and anniversaries, or book holiday time. *But* instead of being focused on civil/secular holidays, the church calendar focuses on the events of holy history (God's mighty acts throughout human history); instead of celebrating national heroes, the church calendar invites us to remember and be thankful for persons of heroic faith (particularly those whose lives are recorded in the Bible); and instead of celebrating national holidays, the church calendar sets aside specific days each year to reflect on some of the great doctrines of Scripture.

How Does the Church Calendar Work?

The church calendar is arranged on the basis of several seasons, but its underlying framework is simply an annual "walk" through the life of Jesus. Let's consider the different seasons in turn.

The church year begins not on January 1 but on the first Sunday of Advent, which falls either in late November or early December. Why? Because Christians, as distinct from the wider culture, have long seen the day set aside to celebrate the birth of the long-awaited Messiah as the appropriate beginning of the year.

Even for the simplest, most casual family birthday celebration, some preparation is required. Since this particular birthday is so important, the wisdom of centuries of Christian practice has been that we need to take time to prepare—hence the season of Advent, the four Sundays before Christmas. The word "advent" means "coming," and consequently the Advent season both looks *back* to the first coming of Jesus at Bethlehem and looks *forward* to his second coming in glory and power. Deliberately and consciously using Advent as a time for reflection on the mighty act of God in the incarnation can be a important tool for individuals and families who want to focus on the real meaning of the birth of Jesus as opposed to the crass commercialization of the "Christmas season" in civil society, which frankly has very little to do with Jesus Christ.

For many evangelicals Christmas is just one day—December 25. But in the church's calendar it is an entire "season." That shouldn't come as a surprise! How could just one day be enough to celebrate the incarnation? The Christmas season runs from Christmas Day until Epiphany (which is set aside to remember the coming of the wise men) on January 6.

After the Christmas season come a number of weeks of "ordinary time." Originally the term "ordinary time" referred to the fact that Sundays in ordinary time were called by ordinal numbers (first, second, third) instead of cardinal (one, two, three) numbers. So one has the first, second, third, and so on Sunday after Epiphany. But one might just as well think of ordinary time in terms of the spiritual reality that while it may be easy to live out one's faith in times of great excitement and celebration—the mountaintop experiences—most of the time we have to live out our following of Jesus in the ordinary, not especially exciting plains or even valleys of life. This period of "ordinary time," however, actually begins with a Sunday set aside to focus on the Baptism of Jesus and ends with a Sunday intended to have us consider the meaning of the Transfiguration of Jesus.

The word "Lent" comes from a Latin term and refers simply to the lengthening of daylight hours in the northern hemisphere in the spring. The Lenten season lasts for forty days, a recollection of the "forty days" Jesus spent in the wilderness being tempted by the devil. (These are forty days *not* counting Sundays, because for Christians, Sunday, as the day of Christ's resurrection, can never be anything but a day of celebration! Every Sunday is a sort of mini-Easter.[2]) Lent is intended to be a solemn time for self-examination. It demands that I think seriously about my following of Jesus. Doing that is usually not very comfortable, for it shows areas where I have been disobedient, parts of life that are not subject to his lordship, and therefore things of which I need to repent. In some churches this kind of solemn reflection and repentance is encouraged by disallowing floral displays and by not singing any choruses, songs, or hymns with the word "Alleluia!" in them. Ash Wednesday is the beginning of the season of Lent. Churches may choose to hold a worship service to mark the beginning of Lent. An ancient custom is for ashes to be placed ("imposed") on the foreheads of those who so wish during this service. This imposition is usually accompanied by words drawn from Scripture such as "Remember, you are dust, and to dust you shall return" (Gen 3:19) or "Repent, and believe the gospel" (Mark 1:15). In the ancient world and throughout the Bible, the wearing of ashes was a well-recognized symbol of public repentance for sin.

The Lenten season draws to an end with the beginning of "Holy Week," so called not because the days of this week are either more ethical or belong more to God than any other days of the year, but because on these days Christians around the world are encouraged to be deeply attentive to the darkest, most serious days of all human history—the last days of the life of Jesus and his execution. This is sometimes called the "passion" of Jesus, from the Greek verb πάσχω, which means "to suffer." Holy Week begins with Palm Sunday, which recalls the triumphant entry of Jesus into Jerusalem, as recorded in the Gospels. In many places worshippers are given palm leaves on this day, and children and choirs may process into the sanctuary waving their palm leaves along with members of the congregation. Some churches may have a worship service on the Wednesday of Holy Week sometimes called "Spy Wednesday." The Christian church is likely the only group in the world—outside of perhaps MI5 or the CIA!—that actually has a spy day! It's a good opportunity for every Christian to ask himself or herself the important and troubling question, "How have I betrayed Jesus?" The Thursday of Holy Week is called "Maundy Thursday." This marks the occasion in the upper room when Jesus celebrated the Passover Meal with his disciples and gave it a new meaning as the Lord's Supper. The word "maundy" is actually an English corruption of the Latin word "mandatum," which means "commandment" and refers to the "new" commandment Jesus gave to his disciples on that night: "I give you a new commandment, that you love one another. Just as I have loved you, you also should love one another" (John 13:34). Here is incredibly rich preaching material. Churches that observe Maundy Thursday usually do so with a worship service that includes the Lord's Supper and sometimes also includes foot washing as a sign of service and love to one another, mimicking the example of Jesus himself as the Gospels record. In many churches, all decorations are removed ("stripped") either on Maundy Thursday or at the Good Friday worship service, as a pointed, visible reminder of the utter emptiness of life apart from God. For churches that regularly use overhead video screens, perhaps this point might be made by deliberately not using them.

Holy Week reaches its blackest, most sorrowful low point on Good Friday. There is a regrettable tendency in some evangelical circles for Good Friday services to be turned into early Easter celebrations. This not only reflects bad theology but also represents a caving in to the ethos of our surrounding secular culture, which wants everything always to be happy, upbeat, and optimistic. But the church's job is not to be a sort of unofficial "jollier upper" for society. The church's message is about truth, truth that, while it can lead to real joy, eternal life, and resurrection, is often not comfortable. I was asked recently why I almost never use standard evangelical phrases such as "Our Lord and Saviour Jesus Christ" or "Is Jesus your personal Saviour?" I almost never use the word "Saviour," only the word "Lord." It isn't merely some oversight or personal quirk. Quite simply it is that Scripture says one cannot have Jesus as Saviour unless he is first Lord. And far too often we want Jesus as Saviour but not as Lord—not really. We want the crown, but we say "thanks but no thanks" to the cross. We want an easy, painless way into the Kingdom, and little change or interference with the way we conduct our day-to-day lives. We would prefer to skip merrily from Palm Sunday to Easter Sunday, and bypass Good Friday. It doesn't work that way. First comes death of self, then life. First comes the *via dolorosa*, the way of sorrows; then, and *only* then, the road that leads to the empty tomb, the Emmaus Road on which the risen Jesus appeared, and the road to the New Jerusalem, when heaven and earth are finally united under the rule, the reign, the lordship of Jesus Christ. The observance of Good Friday in accordance with the church's calendar reinforces all of these important realities.

Finally, after the sorrow of Good Friday comes Easter Sunday, the Sunday of the resurrection! In stark contrast to Western society and the civil calendar, the church's calendar marks Easter *not* Christmas as the most important day. If the birth of Jesus had led to a life that ended on a Roman cross, that birth would have been of little importance. It is the resurrection that set God's stamp of approval on the entire life of Jesus and now marks the critical point of God's great plan to rescue fallen creation. Just like Christmas, Easter in the church calendar is *not* just a one-day event. How could only one day be sufficient to celebrate the resurrection? Easter is a season of *fifty* days, which in the church's calendar is called the "Great Fifty Days" and runs from Easter until Pentecost. During this entire time, the great hymns that celebrate the resurrection are joyously sung Sunday by Sunday. If a congregation uses the lectionary-appointed Scripture lessons (see Lectionary below), readings from the Old Testament are replaced with readings from the book of Acts, the story of the early church. This makes a good deal of sense, for if there had been no resurrection there would have been no church. Toward the end of the Great Fifty Days comes Ascension Day (which may be marked on the closest Sunday). Jesus, having been with the disciples for a number of weeks following the resurrection, now returns to the Father. Here is an opportunity to preach on the meaning of one of the most neglected events in the life of Jesus.

With Pentecost Sunday, a new season begins, albeit a brief season of two Sundays. On Pentecost Sunday Christians are invited to read the story of the coming of the Holy Spirit on the first disciples in Jerusalem a few weeks after the Ascension. The following Sunday, Trinity Sunday, is an opportunity for preaching about one of the most difficult, most neglected, and yet most important of Christian doctrines. Far too often it is possible for an evangelical congregation to go for years without hearing a single sermon devoted to explaining the Trinity and its relevance to daily life. Particularly in Western society where more and more people live alone, have experienced relationship breakdowns, or are separated from family by long distances because of a career, the reality that God is a community of three persons living in mutual, self-giving love and submission is something that needs to be heard!

Now, once again the calendar enters into a period—a very long period—of ordinary time that will last until the church year begins again once more with Advent. There are a few observances of note during this period of ordinary time that churches may choose to mark, each of which provides rich biblical materials for preaching. These include the following:

- *The birth of John the Baptist (June 24).* Jesus said of his cousin John, "among those born of women no one is greater" (Luke 7:28; cf. Matt 11:11). What does John's life say to us about courage, public morality, the identity of Jesus, and doubt?
- *The Virgin Mary (August 15).* For evangelicals who have tended to overreact to Roman Catholic views on Mary to the point of barely mentioning her at all, this is an opportunity to provide solid, biblical teaching and to see Mary as an example of heroic faith.
- *Holy Women of the Old Testament (August 16).* How often have women in the Bible and women of the Old Testament in particular been ignored in evangelical preaching? Here is an opportunity to preach about women such as Miriam, Sarah, Hagar, Deborah, Naomi, Ruth, Esther, and many others.
- *The beheading of John the Baptist (August 29).* Some churches pair this with marking the martyrdoms of Dietrich Bonhoeffer and Maximilian Kolbe by the Nazis during the Second World War. This can be an opportunity to preach about, pray for, and perhaps provide financial assistance to the persecuted church living under oppressive regimes worldwide.
- *Holy Cross Day (September 14).* This is a good opportunity to preach on the meaning of the cross from Scripture.

- *Reformation Sunday (closest Sunday to October 31).* What does it mean to be a Protestant Christian? What differentiates Protestantism from the two other major branches of Christianity (Roman Catholicism and Eastern Orthodoxy)?
- *All Saints' Day (November 1).* What does it mean to be a saint in the biblical sense of that term, which refers to *all* followers of Jesus as saints? What does it mean to say we believe in the "communion of the saints?"
- *Christ the King Sunday.* This observation, the last Sunday of the church's year, is a relatively new observance. It was first instituted, for Roman Catholic Christians, by Pope Pius XI in 1925. This was a period in European history when European political movements and totalitarian governments of both the far right (fascism in Germany, Italy, and Spain) and far left (communism in the Soviet Union) were increasingly making claims to the total allegiance of citizens. Pope Pius wisely recognized that such claims were contrary to the biblical insistence that such allegiance belongs only to Jesus Christ. The observation was established as a pointed reminder of this reality. Recognizing a good thing when they saw it, many Protestant groups rapidly adopted the observation (sometimes also called Reign of Christ Sunday).

Colours of the Church Calendar

There is a long tradition of pairing specific colours with the different seasons or days of the church's calendar. Pulpit hangings, Communion table runners, and banners may use these colours. Like the calendar itself, the colour scheme is not somehow required, nor does it come down to us as from Mount Sinai. It is a tool for teaching, for spiritual growth and formation. Especially in a culture that is increasingly *visually* oriented, this may be a useful tool indeed—even though it is very old.

The most widespread pattern—and there are lots of local variations—is for four colours. *Green*, which represents growth (think gardens, wheat fields) is used during ordinary time. Purple is used during Lent and Advent. *Purple* is a solemn colour, and moreover it is, even today, still the colour used in the robes of kings, which makes it appropriate for marking the time leading to the birth and then the execution of the King of kings. *White* (often trimmed with gold) is used for times of great celebration, notably the seasons of Christmas and Easter. *Red* is used quite rarely—on Pentecost Sunday, on days marking the martyrdom of one of God's servants (for example, John the Baptist), and, in some places, for Reformation Sunday.

The colour red calls to mind the flames, as of fire, on the day of Pentecost, and the blood of those who suffered death rather than deny the faith.

Objections to the Church Calendar

In some evangelical circles, there may be objections raised to using the church calendar. What are these, and how may these concerns be answered?

A frequent objection is that the church calendar is not found in Scripture and, being unbiblical, should not be used. This concern may, if handled well, become a teachable moment about the nature and proper exegesis of the Bible. It is true that the church calendar is not found in Scripture, but then, neither is the automobile that people use to get to church, nor the furnace or the air conditioning in the church building. The Bible also makes no mention of radio, television, or the Internet, even though all of these have greatly facilitated the communication of the gospel worldwide. For that matter, the physical copy of the Bible as a single volume that people hold in their hands is not actually mentioned anywhere in the Bible! The issue then is *not* whether every single thing or practice can be found in the Bible. If we consistently demanded that, then we should all have to walk, ride horses or donkeys, and drive chariots. None of us would have a personal computer, iPod, television, car, refrigeration, electricity, or modern medicine! The question isn't whether something is specifically mentioned in the Bible but whether a thing or practice is in line with the teachings and principles of the Bible. Insofar as the church calendar deepens understanding of the broad sweeping story of salvation, increases knowledge of Scripture and Bible doctrine, and causes people to examine their walk with Christ, repent of sin, and live more obedient lives, then it certainly is in line with the teachings and principles of the Bible.

Others may be quite genuinely anxious that using the church calendar means "observing special days, and months, and seasons, and years" (Gal 4:10) to which the apostle Paul objected. Again, this can be a teachable moment about the importance of context in understanding the Bible (and any other document for that matter). Paul's words are in the context of his condemning the worship of "beings that by nature are not gods" (Gal 4:8), which is certainly *not* the context of the church calendar.

It *is* true that at certain times and in certain places the church calendar *has* been abused. People got into their heads the notions that prayers said or good works performed during a certain season or on certain days were more likely to be answered favourably or regarded more highly by God than on other days. This of course is unbiblical nonsense. But just because something has or might be misused does not mean it is bad in and of itself.

A rather less thoughtful objection is sometimes simply to say that the church calendar is "Catholic" (i.e., Roman Catholic), which in the speaker's mind is somehow a conclusive argument that anything so described should automatically not be employed by Protestant Christians. Pastoral tact combined with firmness will be necessary. Leaving aside the fact that Scripture says *anyone* who confesses Jesus as Lord is a Christian, and therefore to be embraced as a fellow believer rather than automatically disparaged, perhaps one might point out that the calendar is intended to *increase* understanding of the life of Jesus and biblical literacy in general. A bit of humour may help to move the process of understanding along—"Roman Catholics also breathe, drive cars, and take holidays. Should we stop doing those things too?"

Benefits of Using the Church Calendar

Experience suggests that the benefits of using the church calendar far outweigh any drawbacks. Chief among those benefits is that the calendar can be a valuable teaching tool, regularly reminding God's people that they are—and are supposed to be—different from the wider secular culture. What secular Western culture says is true, valuable, or important is often, according to Scripture, untrue, devoid of value, and unimportant. For followers of Jesus, it is the events and major figures of *holy history*, God's unfolding great plan of salvation, which are important. By comparison, events and people of merely local or national importance are insignificant. It is *the* Kingdom, *not* the kingdoms of this world, which is of eternal significance. As Robert Webber comments (with specific reference to the experience of American evangelicals),

> One very obvious form of secularization may be found in most evangelical church calendars. We are organized around . . . the seasonal calendar, the national calendar, and the secular calendar of special days. We celebrate Mother's Day, the Fourth of July, Memorial Day. . . . But when it comes to the sacred seasons of Advent, Christmas, Epiphany, Lent, Holy Week, Easter and Pentecost, we have reduced our celebrations to Christmas Sunday, Good Friday and Easter.[3]

How to Introduce the Use of the Church Calendar

In a congregation that has no history of using the church calendar, it would be pastorally irresponsible (and in some instances pastoral suicide!) suddenly to introduce or impose its use. The people of God deserve better and more respect than that.

Like anything else that is "new," introducing the use of the church calendar requires time and careful teaching/explanation. Begin with the congregation's leaders—both formal and informal (the two are often *not* identical). Before the calendar is introduced to the wider congregation, make sure that the leadership both understands and supports its adoption. Explain what the calendar is and *why* using it would be helpful. Emphasize the underlying structure of the calendar as an annual walk through the life of Jesus and how it can be a tool for improving biblical literacy—things few evangelicals will find objectionable! Do not fail to impress upon your listeners that the calendar is also a tool to help churches avoid being co-opted by the wider, secular culture.

Once the leadership is agreed, the same process needs to be repeated with the whole congregation. Be sure that a "one-time" explanation from the pulpit and/or in a bulletin insert will not be sufficient. Plan instead to explain, frequently, what is happening and why, both orally and in written form, using the bulletin or overhead as a teaching tool. The observation of Advent might be introduced with an announcement on these lines: "Christians realize that the birth of Jesus is of utmost importance. The long-awaited Messiah had finally come. And, more still, that Messiah turned out to be God himself become a human being. Now, nobody knows the exact date of his birth, so eventually Christians picked a date in December to celebrate the birth of Jesus every year. Over the years many folk found that it was a useful spiritual practice to set aside the weeks just before that day to prepare. In our culture, where Jesus gets lost in all the buying and selling, parties, gift giving, and the rest, doesn't that sound like a good idea? *We* know from the Bible that all these material things aren't what Jesus was about. But it's hard not to get caught up in it. So this year we're going to start something new in our church—or at least it's new to us. We're going to observe *Advent*, which means we're actually going to make a conscious effort to focus on what the coming of Jesus really means. The word 'Advent' means 'coming, ' so during the four Sundays in Advent we are invited to look *back* at the first coming of Jesus in Bethlehem, and to look *forward* to his second coming, his second *advent*."

Introducing Lent to an evangelical congregation may be aided with an explanation such as this given by Robert Webber:

> our relationship with God, like a relationship with a spouse, needs to undergo continual renewal and a deepening of commitment. I have found the experience of Lent leads me into a renewal of my spiritual relationship with Jesus Christ. . . . It is a time when I ask myself, "Am I slipping back into the old ways? Is the devil making some inroads into my life . . . ? During Lent, I review my baptismal contract with Christ.[4]

Trinity Sunday might be introduced after this fashion: "One of the most important things we believe about God is summed up in the word 'Trinity.' Unfortunately many Christians have confused or unbiblical ideas about this. So it's a good thing that once every year, the church calendar sets aside a Sunday for us to think about how God is both three and one and what that can possibly have to do with us in day-to-day life." Using these kinds of explanations, regularly and repeatedly, is part of the whole teaching process.

Lectionary

A lectionary is a listing of Scripture passages appointed to be read in a specific order. A lectionary may provide readings for every day of the week or only for Sundays. (The word "lectionary" comes from the Latin word "lection," meaning "reading.")

Contrary to what some evangelicals may think, lectionaries are not something unique to "Catholics" (i.e., Roman Catholics). In fact, Christians have compiled lectionaries from very early in the history of the church, long before there were any such things as Protestantism, Roman Catholicism, and Orthodoxy. Among evangelicals there are numerous popular plans for reading through the Bible once every year (or sometimes every two or three years). In all but name, these schemes are lectionaries.

By long-standing custom, lectionaries that list Scripture passages for each Sunday of the year usually provide four readings (called "lessons")— an Old Testament lesson, a psalm, a reading from one of the letters of the New Testament (usually called "The Epistle"), and last, in the place of honour, a reading from one of the four Gospels. The most widely known and widely used contemporary lectionary is the *Revised Common Lectionary*. It provides Bible readings for each Sunday of the year, taking into account the church calendar with its pattern of seasons and special observances.

The RCL works on a three-year cycle. In Year A, readings from the Gospels focus on Matthew, in Year B on Mark, and in Year C on Luke. (Readings from the Gospel of John are scattered throughout all three years.) If followed faithfully, use of the Revised Common Lectionary exposes congregations to large portions of the entire Bible over a three-year cycle. Like every other thing created by fallen humans, the RCL has limitations. It by no means includes all of the Bible over the three-year cycle. But the reality is that many evangelical churches, having no long-term plan *at all* for Scripture reading on Sundays, end up hearing *far less* of the Bible over the course of any three-year period than they would if they used the RCL. Because it is used so widely across so many denominations,[5] an enormous number of resources tied to the lectionary-appointed readings are available, both in print and online, ranging from Sunday school curricula for all ages to Scripture commentaries. Various online sites provide everything from suggested hymns that tie in with the appointed Scripture readings Sunday by Sunday to artwork suitable for bulletin covers and overheads, which depict or reflect some aspect of the readings.

Using the Revised Common Lectionary and the church calendar will force pastors to preach something much more closely resembling the whole counsel of God as opposed to the parts of Scripture they are most familiar or comfortable with. Together, these two tools help avoid preaching that overemphasizes the particular interests or hobbyhorses of individual pastors. Together, the use of the church calendar and lectionary creates a concrete example of unity with the wider church, with hundreds of millions of Christians reading and thinking about the same texts each Sunday.

Church Calendar and Lectionary Books and Websites

The Library of Vanderbilt Divinity School maintains a superb website (<lectionary.library.vanderbilt.edu>), which has a wealth of resources for the Revised Common Lectionary (and the church calendar). In addition to listing the full text of the prescribed Scripture readings for every Sunday, the site provides suggested wording for prayers for each Sunday that reflect those readings as well as photographs of artworks that connect to the readings. Wesley Theological Seminary's *The Text This Week* (<www.textweek.com>) provides the Scripture texts, plus art, music, and movie indexes, along with links to dozens of Scripture study and sermon sites. Smyth & Helwys offers a weekly blog (<www.nextsunday.com/coracle/>) that often has useful resources. Thom Shuman, a Presbyterian pastor and poet, is responsible for <lectionaryliturgies.blogspot.com>, which provides thoughtful calls to worship, collects, prayers of confession, and commissionings that align with the RCL-appointed Scripture readings.

The three-volume *Texts for Preaching: A Lectionary Commentary, Based on the NRSV* provides commentary on every lesson for each Sunday in the Revised Common Lectionary cycle,[6] and counts the inestimable Old Testament scholar Walter Brueggemann among its editors. A similar approach is taken in the series titled *Preaching through the Christian Year*, written by noted preacher Fred Craddock together with John H. Hayes, Carl R. Holladay, and Gene M. Tucker.[7] Both series are available as printed books and on CD rom. An interesting contribution is the *Ancient Christian Devotional*[8] series published by Inter Varsity. The approach is devotional rather than exegetical. The Scripture readings from the Revised Common Lectionary are paired with comments from some of the early church's most notable figures such as Augustine, Chrysostom, Origen, Athanasius, and Hilary of Poitiers.

Understanding Secular Culture

Those who are responsible for leading common worship, and particularly those responsible for preaching, can hardly expect to teach God's people how to live out the faith in a countercultural way, as a minority, if they do not themselves have a deep understanding of the secular view of life. In this respect, understanding or properly exegeting the culture is just as necessary as understanding and properly exegeting the Scriptures. Paraphrasing Karl Barth, one must lead common worship and preach with the Bible in one hand and the day's news feed in the other.

Some may question the need for the newspaper. Isn't the Bible enough? We don't need anything else! There are several problems with this objection to knowing the culture. Most serious of all is that for all intents and purposes it denies the incarnation. In the end, God did not just give commandments from on high as at Mount Sinai, nor did he just send prophets to convey his messages. In the end, instead of standing apart from humanity, God *became* a human being. How then can we justify standing apart from the world, perhaps even being proud of our ignorance of it? That is most emphatically not the model that we see in the incarnation! Second, this objection seems to assume that *everything* in human society is bad or evil, and real Christians should therefore separate themselves from it. But in fact the Bible itself is quite clear that there is both good *and* evil in the world, both wheat *and* tares. Humanity is fallen and sinful, but we are not totally depraved—we are not as bad or evil as it is possible to be in every aspect of life. There *is* good in this world. Third, for those who lead worship, and especially for those who preach, to be ignorant of the surrounding culture is to fail the people of God who come, week by week, to participate in common worship. C. S. Lewis preached a sermon at the University Church of St. Mary the Virgin in Oxford, just after the onset of the Second World War, that he titled "Learning in Wartime." Lewis said,

> If all the world were Christian, it might not matter if all the world were uneducated. But, as it is, a cultural life will exist outside the Church whether it exists inside or not. To be ignorant . . . now . . . would be . . . to betray our uneducated brethren who have, under God, no defence but us against the intellectual attacks of the heathen.[9]

We probably wouldn't use the term "heathen" today, and we certainly don't propose that the "brethren" should remain uneducated, but the point remains valid. Is it not the particular and sacred responsibility of worship leaders and preachers to protect and defend the flock? How is that to be done if there is no knowledge of the enemy? And even more so, how is the flock to be equipped to give a reason for the hope it professes (cf. 1 Pet 3:15) if it cannot make itself understood by those to whom that reason is being given?

For those who lead common worship and those who preach, understanding the culture must be a never-ending, constant job. Of course the question is where and how even to begin such thinking, study, and reflection. There are many entry points to this undertaking. Here are a few resources that may prove helpful.

History

A basic understanding of how we got where we are is a good place to begin. This will involve a particular emphasis on intellectual history—the history of ideas. Over time, ideas—the pen—really is mightier than the sword. Some books that will likely prove helpful include the following:

- Owen Chadwick, *The Secularization of the European Mind in the Nineteenth Century* (1975; repr., Cambridge: Cambridge University Press, 2000). This volume looks at both the social and intellectual processes involved in secularization in nineteenth-century Western Europe.

Chadwick was a professor of history for many years at Cambridge University, England, where he also held the office of Vice-Chancellor. For a decade he was Chancellor of the University of East Anglia. A former president of the British Academy, Chadwick was also appointed a Knight Commander of the Order of the British Empire and a member of the Order of Merit.

• Gerald R. Cragg, *The Church & The Age of Reason 1648–1789*, The Pelican History of the Church, vol. 4, ed. Owen Chadwick (Harmondsworth, England: Penguin, reprinted with revisions, 1976; repr., 1983). This is a good overview of church history in Western, Central, and Eastern Europe during the period of the Enlightenment, from the Peace of Westphalia to the onset of the French Revolution. Cragg, a Canadian clergyman and scholar, served rural, town, and city churches before appointment as professor of theology at McGill University, Montreal. He then was appointed Professor of Ecclesiastical History at Andover-Newton Theological Seminary, just outside Boston.

• Peter Gay, *The Enlightenment: An Interpretation—The Rise of Modern Paganism* (1966; repr., New York: W. W. Norton & Company, 1995) and Peter Gay, *The Enlightenment: An Interpretation—The Science of Freedom* (1969; repr. New York: W. W. Norton & Company, 1995). Together, this pair of books provides a detailed but enjoyably readable account of the Enlightenment in Western Europe, covering everything from science and politics to education, art, and ethics. Readers meet the major thinkers (philosophes as Gay calls them) of the Enlightenment. While they often come across as simplistic and vastly overconfident about the place and possibilities of reason and the empirical method, at the same time their contributions to much of what we value in modern liberal democracy are also recognized. After teaching for several years at Columbia, Gay joined the faculty of Yale University as Professor of History. He is currently Sterling Professor of History Emeritus at Yale.

• George M. Marsden and Bradley J. Longfield, eds., *The Secularization of the Academy* (New York: Oxford University Press, 1992). In eleven essays, the contributors explore how Christianity in Britain, Canada, and the United States went from being a leading player in higher education to being a peripheral, even excluded player.

• Martin Marty, *The Modern Schism: Three Paths to the Secular* (Eugene OR: Wipf and Stock, 2012). Martin Marty is one of the most distinguished American church historians. Originally published in 1969, this slim volume (191 pages) argues that secularism in the Western world took three distinct forms. In continental Western Europe, especially in France, secularism took the form of outright attack on faith and the institutions of faith. In Britain, by contrast, secularism took the form of a slow drifting away from faith, while in the United States, the old theological and religious terminology was retained, but the meanings were changed such that they are often no longer Christian but secular.

- Hugh McLeod, *Secularisation in Western Europe, 1848–1914* (London: MacMillan, 2000). McLeod was the Professor of Church History at Birmingham University, England, and a leader in the field of secularization studies. This study focuses on the development of secularization in Germany, France, and England, arguing that its causes, nature, and progress (or lack thereof) was extremely varied.

- Wade Rowland, *Galileo's Mistake: The Archaeology of a Myth—Why Science Rules and Why It Shouldn't* (Toronto: Thomas Allen, 2001). Dr. Wade Rowland is a former journalist and is currently Professor of Communications at Toronto's York University. Rowland argues that the widely held interpretation of Galileo's trial by the church in 1633 is simplistic and inaccurate. Using an engaging combination of detailed historical work and fictional dialogues, he builds a strong case that Galileo and the Church were in fact arguing over something far more important than whether the earth revolved around the sun or vice-versa. The real issue had to do with truth and how human beings can know it. Rowland insists that while religion has room for including science as a way of finding truth, science at least as the Enlightenment thinkers defined it allows no room for any way of discovering truth other than itself.

Modernism and Postmodernism

The secular approach to life in the Western world essentially has two major underlying intellectual streams: modernism and postmodernism. Those who lead common worship need to be familiar with both.

Modern thought is usually traced to the period called the Enlightenment, the era in Western intellectual history from the late seventeenth to the late eighteenth centuries. Although extremely diverse in their ideas, those identified with the movement had identifiably common goals, including the reform of society using reason, and challenging long-held ideas based on tradition or faith. Leaders of the movement opposed religious and political intolerance, which were both widespread, attacked superstitious beliefs, also widespread, and criticized abuses of power by absolute monarchs and the frequently closely allied state churches. They insisted on a vast increase in personal freedoms and respect for human rights—values that we continue to hold dear today. A few Enlightenment leaders espoused atheism. Many more—including many of the "founding fathers" of the United States—were deists.[10] (Deists believed that God had created the world, established unalterable "laws of nature" by which it operated, and thereafter did not interfere in the creation. God was an "absentee watchmaker." Among other things this view meant that miracles, notably the incarnation, were impossible.) Major Enlightenment thinkers included Denis Diderot, Montesquieu, Voltaire, Baruch Spinoza, Immanuel Kant, John Locke, Matthew Tindal, Thomas Hobbes, Issac Newton, David Hume, and Thomas Paine. The single most important distinguishing feature of Enlightenment thought was that it commonly insisted that the *only* way to know anything was by means of the empirical method. Essentially, if something could not be tasted, touched, heard, seen, or smelled, it didn't exist (or at least, if it did exist, it was unimportant). This stands in stark contrast to the Christian view that valid knowledge can be obtained *both* by empirical investigation *and* divine revelation. Although many modern thinkers claimed to be extremely open minded, a question can be raised as to who is truly more open minded: the "modern" thinker who insists in advance that there is only one way of obtaining knowledge, or the person who is at least open to the possibility of obtaining knowledge from revelation as well as from empirical observation! Even though it tends toward becoming a rant, frequently deviates from its announced subject, and is riddled with logical contradictions and historical errors, Richard Dawkin's *The God Delusion* is a widely read and popular contemporary exposition of modernism (in an aggressively atheistic form).

Postmodern thought may be understood as a reaction to the overweening claims made for human reason and the empirical method by modern/Enlightenment thought. Major figures include Martin Heidegger, Jacques Derrida, and Michel Foucault. Whether the movement represents a genuine sea change in Western thought and whether postmodernism has any long-term staying power is unlikely to be clear for many decades. Regardless of its prospects, however, postmodern thought is at present a major influence in many university faculties, particularly in the arts, fine arts, and education. Many of the chief figures in postmodern thought write in extremely dense and difficult forms. A much easier entre to postmodern thought is *The Elegance of the Hedgehog,* a novel written by French philosophy professor Muriel Barbery.[11] This deliciously rich story is the tale of a twelve-year-old girl who lives in a Paris apartment building and the building's fifty-something concierge. Both, as it turns out, have a secret—they are highly intelligent but don't want anyone to know. This novel in fact provides much insight not just into contemporary French society but also into postmodern thought and attitudes in general.

Postmodern thinkers insist that it is not possible to have an overarching story ("meta-narrative") that describes reality. All that is possible are our individual or group narratives. Asserting that there is a meta-narrative is nothing more than oppression. It is an imperialistic attempt to impose your views and opinions or the views and opinions of your group on everyone else. (At a basic level, postmodernism is self-contradictory. If there are no meta-narratives *except* that there are no meta-narratives, that means there is at least one meta-narrative. Further, if you or your group is of the opinion that there are no meta-narratives, then it is a form of oppression, is it not, to try to impose that opinion on another?) Although first published in 1943, decades before the postmodern school of thought was called such, *The Abolition of Man* by C. S. Lewis, is a short, well-argued response to postmodernism. The late Stanley J. Grenz's *A Primer on Postmodernism*[12] is a scholarly introduction to postmodern thought and a response to it from a broadly evangelical perspective.

Sociology

A number of sociologists of religion have contributed significantly to our understanding of secularism in Western society. Outstanding are the following:

- Peter Berger, Grace Davie, and Effie Fokas, *Religious America, Secular Europe? A Theme and Variations* (Farnham, Surrey: Ashgate Publishing, 2008). This volume argues that the old thesis that modernity leads inevitably to secularism is inaccurate; modernity can come in both secular (European) and religious (United States) models. While the religiosity of the general American population (though not its cultural elite, which is deeply secular) is unusual in the Western world, it is not unusual in terms of the world as a whole. Instead, deeply secular Western Europe is the exception.
- James Davison Hunter, *Culture Wars: The Struggle to Define America—Making Sense of the Battles over the Family, Art, Education, Law and Politics* (New York: BasicBooks, 1991). Hunter is Distinguished Professor of Religion, Culture, and Social Theory at the University of Virginia. He argues that there have been three major cultural divisions in Western history, that between Jew and Gentile, between Protestant and Roman Catholic, and, today, the most important division of all, between those who believe there

is a transcendent reality (God) who defines what is good, right, and beautiful and those who do not. This most recent cultural divide has resulted in what, until fairly recently, would have been unheard of alliances, such as evangelical Protestants, traditional Roman Catholics, orthodox Jews, and others making common cause on a variety of hot-button issues in the public square.

• Bryan R. Wilson, *Religion in Secular Society: A Sociological Comment* (1966; repr., Middlesex, England: Penguin, 1969). Wilson was Reader in Sociology at the University of Oxford, a founding member of the University Association for the Sociology of Religion, and President of the International Society for the Sociology of Religion. He argues that secularism in Europe took the form of people no longer going to church, but in the United States, it took the form of co-opting the churches.

Theology and Biblical Studies

A number of contemporary theologians and biblical scholars are strongly focused on doing theology and interpreting the Bible for and in the context of a secular society. Notables include Old Testament scholar Walter Brueggemann, Canadian theologian Douglas John Hall, Duke University's Stanley Hauwerwas, and Roger E. Olson, a Baptist clergyman and professor at Truett Theological Seminary at Baylor University.

Ongoing Awareness

Because we live within Western society, it is often difficult to stand outside it, and see how and in what ways it is in contradiction to the Kingdom Jesus talked about, and how and in what ways evangelicals have been co-opted by secularity. How can we go about doing this?

• *Internet Resources.* Though there is a great deal of claptrap on the Internet, some sites provide thoughtful insights to secular society and the relationship of evangelicals to it. Consider in particular Facebook sites such as Sojourners Magazine and Liberal Evangelicals. The mission of the Institute for the Study of Secularism in Society and Culture, located at Trinity College, Hartford, Connecticut, is to advance the understanding of the role of secular values and the process of secularization itself in contemporary society. It takes a multidisciplinary, non-partisan, and non-denominational approach. The Institute's webpage is found at <www.trincoll.edu/Academics/centers/isssc/Pages/default.aspx>. The Centre for Christianity and Culture at Regent's Park College has produced a series of volumes, programmes, and other resources that aim at bringing a specifically Christian perspective to contemporary life and thought. Regent's Park College, a Baptist foundation, is a permanent private hall of Oxford University. The Centre for Christianity and Culture is found as part of the Regent's Park College website: <www.rpc.ox.ac.uk>. The London Institute for Contemporary Christianity, founded by John Stott, has a variety of interesting resources on its website: <www.licc.org.uk>.

- *Listening to Christians from outside the Western world.* Despite the dominance of Western culture worldwide, our sisters and brothers who live in other parts of the world are often able to "see" things that we cannot. Make it a practice to read theological writing from the developing world. Connect with recent immigrants and refugees and seek out their knowledge.
- *Reading the "poets."* Dr. Harold L. Mitton, former principal of Acadia Divinity College and lecturer in homiletics, told his students, "If you want to know what is really going on in a society, read its 'poets.'" Those "poets" include everything from books penned by contemporary writers to recent plays and movies.
- *Subscribing to a good news source.* One excellent choice is *The Guardian Weekly*. In a news environment dominated by ten-second sound bites and wire reports, *The Guardian Weekly* stands out as a bastion of in-depth investigation and reporting. Frequently it reveals the dark side of the foreign and economic policies of Western nations. *Sojourners* magazine, edited by Jim Wallis, is a reliable source for matters pertaining to social justice, usually written from a broadly evangelical perspective. Their online site is <www.sojo.net>.

Evangelism/Mission/Outreach in a Secular Context

For some evangelicals it will be disorienting to think about evangelism *apart* from Sunday morning worship. Largely eliminating the "altar call" from common worship raises the question, "How then do we do evangelism? How do we spread the gospel?" The simple answer of course is that we return to the model of the New Testament, where witness/outreach/evangelism happened in daily life as believers talked about and lived out their faith, and in the public marketplace as when Paul spoke in the marketplace and areopagus in Athens, or in a lecture hall in Corinth. Three books that will especially stimulate thinking about doing evangelism in a secular culture—outside of common worship—are the following:

- Stuart Murray, *The Church after Christendom* (Milton Keynes: Pater Noster, 2004). Murray is the chair of the UK Anabaptist Network and the editor of *Anabaptism Today*. He also oversees Urban Expression, an urban church-planting agency. This book is a study of the state of the church in the United Kingdom, but much of what it says applies also to the Canadian and American situation. Stuart argues that much of the way in which we "do" church is infected with the Christendom model, that churches must recognize there are many different ways of being secular, and that for many people today, their way to faith in Christ will be slow process of "belonging" *before* "believing."
- Gary V. Nelson, *Borderland Churches: A Congregation's Introduction to Missional Living* (St. Louis: Chalice Press, 2008). Nelson, currently President of Tyndale University College and Seminary in Toronto, previously served as General Secretary of Canadian Baptist Ministries and Vice President of the Baptist World Alliance. This extremely accessible read discusses how churches and individuals can enter into the "borderlands," defined as places and situations where Christian faith and non-faith (secularism) or other faiths intersect.
- Ronald Rolheiser, ed., *Secularity and the Gospel: Being Missionaries to Our Children* (New York: Crossroad, 2006). Rolheiser, a Roman Catholic priest, is president of the Oblate School of Theology in San Antonio, Texas. He is profoundly distressed by how the church is "losing ground within secular culture," particularly among the children of Christians who no longer are connected with the church. The volume focuses on how "to become missionaries again within our own culture."

Worship Manuals

Hundreds of worship manuals are available to worship leaders. Many are denominationally specific, while others, even if they may be produced by a specific denomination, are much broader in approach. Some are organized, at least in part, by taking into account the seasons and observations of the church calendar. The quality varies widely. What is important is that any worship manual be clearly informed by a biblical theology of worship *and* that it be cognizant of the reality of the secular culture in which we are called to live out our faith.

Two of the best such manuals are *The Worship Sourcebook*,[13] jointly published by the Calvin Institute of Christian Worship, Faith Alive Christian Resources, and Baker Book House, and *Gathering for Worship: Patterns and Prayers for the Community of Disciples*,[14] published by Canterbury Press for The Baptist Union of Great Britain. Both come with a jacket inside the cover containing a CD version of the book.

Both of these volumes are committed to the biblical fourfold pattern of worship and are strongly influenced by evangelical and Reformed theological traditions. Each provides complete orders of service for Sunday common worship, suggested wording for calls to worship, prayers of praise, confession, thanksgiving, and intercession, responses and the like, as well as patterns for the celebration of both Holy Communion and Baptism (in the case of the first work, for both adult and infant baptism, in the case of the latter, not surprisingly only for adult baptism). Both also provide materials suitable for the major seasons of the church calendar.

Other Website Resources for Worship

Two other websites also deserve mention for providing easy access to a wide array of resources for those who are serious about common worship that follows the fourfold pattern of Scripture, reflects historic evangelical emphases, and resists being secularized:

- <iws.edu>. The Institute for Worship Studies was established in the 1990s by Robert Webber. The institute offers graduate study in worship, and the website provides a huge worship bibliography.
- <worship.calvin.edu>. This is the site for the Calvin Institute of Church Worship, which organizes an annual conference on worship and publishes books on a variety of subjects, such as moving a church from maintenance to mission, worldwide Christian music, art and faith, the small church, and the psalms in worship.

Conclusion

In the preface to this book I issued a warning—*caveat lector*, let the reader beware. It is my profound hope and prayer that evangelicals will indeed become aware of the enormous danger we face in Western society of becoming secularized, mere chaplains to the wider culture, oblivious to the contradictions between what our secular culture says is real and important and what Scripture says is real and important. The resources exist within our tradition, I believe, to step back from the abyss. But that step back will only happen if, recognizing the danger, we make a firm, unwavering, and conscious decision to insure that our common worship is focused exclusively on the God whom we know best in Jesus Christ. Such worship, by its very nature, will be, as it always has been, countercultural. This is my plea to my fellow evangelicals.

Notes

1. Ben Witherington III, *We Have Seen His Glory: A Vision of Kingdom Worship*, in Calvin Institute of Christian Worship Liturgical Studies Series, ed. John D. Witvliet (Grand Rapids MI: Eerdmans, 2010) 151.

2. This is why it was and still remains uncommon to have funeral services on Sundays.

3. Robert E. Webber, *Worship Is a Verb: Celebrating God's Mighty Deeds of Salvation* (Peabody MA: Hendrickson, 2004) 6.

4. Ibid., 167.

5. The Revised Common Lectionary was initially compiled by leaders and scholars from multiple denominations, both Roman Catholic and Protestant. The Protestant denominations included the Anglican Church of Canada, Christian Church (Disciples of Christ), Christian Reformed Church in North America, the Episcopal Church (United States), Evangelical Lutheran, Free Methodist Church of Canada, the Lutheran Church-Missouri Synod, Presbyterian Church (USA), Presbyterian Church (Canada), Reformed Church in America, United Church of Canada, United Churches of Christ, and the United Methodist Church. Many Protestant denominations not involved in the initial process of compiling the lectionary have since joined the ongoing revision process and adopted its use. The RCL is now widely used in churches ranging from the American Baptist Convention, the Evangelical Free Covenant Church, and among many Wesleyans to the Church of the Brethren. The RCL is also now widely used outside Canada and the United States.

6. Walter Brueggemann, Charles B. Cousar, Beverly R. Gaventa, and James D. Newsome, eds., *Texts for Preaching: A Lectionary Commentary Based on the NRSV, Vol. 1: Year A* (1995); *Vol. 2: Year B* (1993); and *Vol. 3: Year C* (1994).

7. Fred B. Craddock, John H. Hayes, Carl R. Holladay, and Gene M. Tucker, *Preaching through the Christian Year: A* (New York: Bloomsbury T & T Clark, 1992); *B* (1993); and *C* (1994).

8. Cindy Crosby and Thomas C. Oden, *Ancient Christian Devotional: A Year of Weekly Readings, Lectionary Cycle A* (Downers Grove IL, InterVarsity, 2007); *Cycle B* (2011); and *Cycle C* (2009).

9. C. S. Lewis, "Learning in Wartime," in *Fern-seed and Elephants and Other Essays on Christianity*, ed. Walter Hooper (Glasgow: Fountain, 1977) 34.

10. Widespread scholarly debate continues about George Washington's beliefs. Perhaps this is not surprising given that, even during his own lifetime, many of those closely associated with him were divided about whether Washington was a Christian or a deist, or perhaps something vaguely between the two. Washington did attend the Episcopal Church, but somewhat sporadically. Thomas Jefferson, principal author of the Declaration of Independence and third president of the United States, was very clearly a deist and held fiercely anti-clerical opinions. Late in life Jefferson even created his own version of the Bible by literally cutting and pasting sections of the New Testament with scissors and glue. This resulting work excluded all references to the miracles of Jesus, the resurrection, and all texts

that suggest Jesus was divine. Like many deists, Jefferson saw religion as a matter of ethics and morals, not as doctrine or a worldview that described reality. Benjamin Franklin, also vehemently anti-clerical, declared himself to be a deist in his autobiography. He went so far, during a visit to Paris, as to ask Voltaire, the French deist, to "bless" his grandson. James Madison, the fourth president, who was instrumental in drafting the American Constitution and wrote the Bill of Rights, while formally an Episcopalian, made few references to his personal convictions but was known to be an avid reader of English deist tracts. Alexander Hamilton, author of the majority of the hugely influential *Federalist Papers* and the first secretary of the treasury, started as an orthodox evangelical who appears who have moved gradually toward some form of deism. Thomas Paine authored the influential revolutionary tract *The Age of Reason*. The first part of the tract included an attack on revealed religion, Paine's own list of what he regarded as inconsistencies in the Bible, and his case for deism. In the tract, Paine professed his belief in one God but denied any belief in an afterlife and insisted that the only duty of humans was to act justly and kindly toward one another.

11. Muriel Barbery, *The Elegance of the Hedgehog*, trans. Alison Anderson (New York: Europa Editions, 2008).

12. Stanley J. Grenz, *A Primer on Postmodernism* (Grand Rapids MI: Eerdmans, 1996).

13. Carrie Titcombe Steenwyk and John D. Witvliet, eds., *The Worship Sourcebook*, 2nd ed. (Grand Rapids MI: Calvin Institute of Christian Worship, Faith Alive Christian Resources, Baker Books, 2013).

14. Christopher J. Ellis and Myra Blyth, eds., *Gathering for Worship: Patterns and Prayers for the Community of Disciples* (Norwich, England: Canterbury Press, 2005; repr., 2007).